W9-BCX-651

$8.95

Clarinet & Saxophone Experience

Stanley Richmond

This manual is one of the most comprehensive ever written on the clarinet and saxophone family.

In simple, uncluttered terms, the author provides a detailed description of the theory, mechanism and adjustment of the two instruments and goes on to show how important the knowledge of these is for intonation, tone control and general technical facility.

Acoustics, embouchure, fingering alternatives, reed selection and scraping, tricks of transposition and the use of accessories are just a few of the items discussed in this highly informative work.

A detailed contents list is provided for quick reference and the book is filled with musical examples, tables and illustrations. The result is a permanently useful handbook for the beginner and the professional musician.

Clarinet and Saxophone Experience

Clarinet and Saxophone Experience

STANLEY RICHMOND

DARTON, LONGMAN & TODD, LONDON
ST MARTIN'S PRESS, NEW YORK

First published in Great Britain in 1972
by Darton, Longman & Todd Ltd
85 Gloucester Road, London SW7 4SU
and in U.S.A. by St Martin's Press Inc.
175 Fifth Avenue, New York, NY 10010
© 1972 Stanley Richmond
Printed in Great Britain by Butler and Tanner Ltd
Frome and London

ISBN 0 232 51148 9

Library of Congress catalogue card no: 70-183051

CONTENTS

v

Chapter 6   96

Chapter 7   110

ILLUSTRATIONS

MUSIC EXAMPLES

TABLES

FINGERING TABLES

OTHER TABLES

MEASUREMENT CONVERSIONS

Instrument measurements are quoted on different scales, which makes comparison impossible unless some are converted.

Millimetres to inches		Inches to millimetres	
0.1 mm	0.004 inch	0.050 inch	1.27 mm
0.2	0.008	0.1	2.54
0.3	0.012	0.15	3.81
0.4	0.016	0.2	5.08
0.5	0.020	0.25	6.35
0.6	0.024	0.3	7.62
0.7	0.028	0.35	8.89
0.8	0.031	0.4	10.16
0.9	0.035	0.45	11.43
1	0.039	0.5	12.7
2	0.079	0.55	13.97
3	0.118	0.6	15.24
4	0.157	0.65	16.51
5	0.197	0.7	17.78
6	0.236	0.75	19.05
7	0.276	0.8	20.32
8	0.315	0.85	21.59
9	0.354	0.9	22.86
10	0.394	0.95	24.13
11	0.433	1	25.4
12	0.472		
13	0.512	*Fractions*	
14	0.551	1/64 inch	0.4 mm
15	0.590	1/32	0.79
16	0.630	1/16	1.59
17	0.670	1/8	3.17
18	0.709	1/4	6.35
19	0.748	1/2	12.7
20	0.787	9/16	14.29
21	0.827	19/32	15.08
22	0.866	5/8	15.87
23	0.905	21/32	16.67
24	0.945	11/16	17.46
25	0.984	23/32	18.26
26	1.024	3/4	19.05

PREFACE

Clarinet and saxophone instruments need maintenance after manufacture by servicing in several ways, and for this the player is responsible. The reed and mouthpiece are often accepted as troublesome items, because making the choice of a mouthpiece and/or barrel from those offered requires more than a superficial consideration.

In addition to establishing the suitability of mouthpiece, reed and barrel for both instrument and player, reliable decisions on the keywork, its adjustments and fingering, are vital.

There has been little information made available for the general study of these fundamental issues, and instruments have not improved to keep pace with the times. More time is probably spent in learning to use the keywork of the clarinet than that of any other instrument, and players take years of experience before being able to make the decisions which give them individual advantage in musical and technical performance.

Playing the clarinet or saxophone involves knowing what can be done to bring it to, and maintain it in, its best condition.

This book brings together the many aspects involved in full and accurate control of the instruments. It gives the reader all the information and explanations which enable instrumental failings to be understood and remedied. It is hoped that they will offer a new approach to eliminating playing hazards encountered by musically proficient players as well as by the less experienced.

The basic relationship between the sound-producing unit and other instrument parts is commonly given insufficient consideration. Important dimensions therefore are reviewed for matching parts to each other and to the notes of the instruments. Fine tuning, specific keywork positions for personal needs and other essential adjustments are dealt with and illustrated.

The adjustments quoted enable players to appreciate what degree of improvement these might give to their instrumental ability, whether choosing to direct an instrument adjuster or to undertake adjustments themselves.

The respective chapters include tables and examples of alternative and extended-range fingerings, transposition and playing effects, which all facilitate performance of the highest standard. It is hoped that in this practical handbook all clarinet and saxophone musicians, the player, the teacher and the progressive pupil, whatever their style of music, will find welcome aids to their musical accomplishment.

1972   *Stanley Richmond*

INTRODUCTION

Sound. Decibels. Hertz. Temperature.
Pitch. Transmission. Forming notes.
Harmonics. The scale.

SOUND

Since sound production will in one way or another be the theme throughout this book, it seems fitting to begin with a brief introduction containing some relevant acoustic information. Some readers will doubtless already be familiar with the application of acoustics in instruments, but even they may perhaps not realise just how much an understanding can be applied in making a critical assessment of an instrument, or in getting an instrument into its best and easiest-playing condition.

What we hear as sound is in fact the energy from vibrations or impulses which reaches our eardrums. Weak sound of any kind may be so weak as to be inaudible to the human ear, but if the intensity is gradually increased the sound will come to the point of being heard. It is then said to have reached the threshold of audibility and this level of sound is termed the zero of intensity.

DECIBELS

From this point, the strength of a sound (or level of sound) is expressed in units of decibels (abbreviated as dB). Decibels are not the measurement for the absolute intensity of sound, but only for the relative intensity of that which is heard, so they are used as an indication of differences of intensity to the ear. Under good conditions, in the absence of disturbance by other sound, 1 decibel is said to be just detectable by the ear. The upper limit is reached when sound intensity is so great that it enters the threshold of painful intensity at 140 decibels (dB).

1

Decibels are also used to measure another characteristic of instrumental sound: generation of the sound.

Although to the casual listener it might appear that any note from an instrument begins instantaneously, this is not really so. It takes a very small though still measurable amount of time for a note to build up from zero decibels to its full strength. This short space of time is called the 'duration of the transients' and is measured in milliseconds (abbreviated ms). This measurement is obviously a matter of instrument design, and although it varies a great deal between different kinds of instrument, it even varies between instruments of the same kind according to their design and playing condition. For comparative purposes these differences are expressed as a rate of increase in sound level per second of time, that is to say, in decibels per second (abbreviated dB/s). This rate of increase in sound level is talked of as though it had been plotted on a graph—which indeed it could be—and where the rate is fast the 'slope' for one second of the transient attack would be shown pronounced or steep, while a mellow sound with a slow rate of increase would show a more gentle slope. Instruments which produce a fast rate of increase are said to have a percussive attack, but this applies to the instrument and not the efforts of a player.

HERTZ

All sound involves vibration both to develop it and for its reception by the ear—the frequency of the vibration directly controls and may be used to describe the pitch of the sound heard. The frequency is expressed in the number of impulses per second of time, by the unit hertz (abbreviated as Hz). So 1 Hz means one vibrational impulse per second. Not that the ear would ever hear such a slowly repeated impulse or frequency as a sound. The lowest sound that is audible as a note to the ear needs at least 20 to 25 impulses per second to create a very low note indeed (below piano range). As the frequency of impulses increases from this low limit so does the pitch of audible sound, until it reaches the highest limit of human audibility, which is in the region of 15,000 to 20,000 Hz according to personal limits for both ends of the scale. This is simplified by saying that very slow vibrations do not excite our eardrums fast enough to create sound and very fast vibrations are too fast for eardrums to identify as sound.

TEMPERATURE

The frequency of 440 Hz gives the pitch of note A used familiarly in setting up the pitch of many musical instruments, but in speaking of instrumental pitch there are factors to be taken into consideration, such as humidity and temperature of the air in and around the instrument, which disturb this precise control. At a given temperature sound travels through the air at a constant speed and reaches the ear at a frequency calculated to produce a note of a specific pitch, but if the air is at a higher temperature, or is more humid due to a higher water content, the sound travels a little faster, that is, at a higher frequency of vibration. This raises the pitch and a higher note is heard.

This variability of pitch by temperature sets quite a problem for instrumentalists, because some instruments react to changes of air temperature in the opposite way from others. Wind instruments, notably those in the brass section, rise in pitch with a rise in temperature, whereas the pitch of stringed instruments, including the piano, falls. It is for this reason that the pitch tuning of instruments has to be specified at a given temperature and this has been fixed as 20°C (68°F) since 1939 for the International Standard Pitch of musical instruments at A 440 Hz. However, there has been a tendency towards higher pitch—for use in both Europe and America, instruments are now made at the pitch of A 442 Hz and from these areas there are reports of even higher playing pitch being used. This is too high for clarinets of the A 440 Hz pitch level.

PITCH

Previous to this international agreement there was a pitch termed 'low pitch' which was of almost the same frequency at 439 Hz and this was known also as 'New Philharmonic' pitch. This must not be confused with an even earlier pitch called 'Old Philharmonic' which was a high pitch of A 452 Hz. Brass and military bands played at this pitch for years after orchestras and pianos were changed to the lower one, a situation which created pitch chaos for players, when making a change of instrument or playing ensemble. Older pipe organs, as distinct from the more recently built ones and the electronic types, are still to be found using this high pitch, so this is a point which must be established prior to any attempt at playing in ensemble with an organ or indeed any other instrument.

Apart from the aural-musical method of checking the pitch of instrumental notes, by comparison with another reliable source such as a tuning fork or pipe, there are electrical methods of doing this, such as the stroboscope or the calibrated cathode-ray oscilloscope, which give a visual indication of whether the number of vibrations per second in a tone is technically correct at the time of checking, but the variations of other times and conditions under which instruments must be used preclude this technicality from superseding the former method.

TRANSMISSION

Sound transmits through air and other mediums of gas, liquid or solid. Incidentally, the speed of sound (velocity) varies in the different mediums through which it passes and there are reflective and refractory changes not being considered here. However, the speed through air is only one quarter of that in water, so the frequency of vibrations can be affected by water in instruments. Sound is made up of only those vibrations which travel longitudinally in the direction of the sound progression or transmission, and this can be shown by referring to the principle of a sound-producing loud-speaker. The speaker diaphragm vibrates forwards and backwards to re-create sound in a very efficient way. These vibrations oscillate the air particles in front of (and behind) the diaphragm of the speaker, by a direct push outwards and a pull return.

From this it is easy to see that in the case of the reed and air column instruments, the longitudinal movement might be similar to that of the loud-speaker principle, although the vibrations are started by the reed from one end of the pipe. Alternating frequencies of outward and return progressions mentioned above are really best visualised in the case of instruments as a frequency and its reflection of opposite movement, but otherwise alike because they originate from the same source. These movements do not cancel each other out as might be supposed because the reflection is one of vibration with a time lag of an end-of-tube reaction involved.

Within the confines of the instrument pipe a 'stationary wave' of push and counter push, as described, is developed. Technically, a stationary wave is formed by two progressive 'waves' of the same frequency of vibration, passing through each other in opposite directions. This development of frequencies is perhaps more aptly described by its other name, a 'standing wave', since within itself it is full of many different vibrations formed by the combination of the two forces.

FORMING NOTES

Sound is made up of reciprocals freely called 'waves', but these would seem to be represented more clearly as 'combinations of vibrations'. So far these are already known by the Hz specification of vibration-frequency and time, but there is also a length measurement of the reciprocal (wave) to be dealt with in the section on harmonics. For the moment width is very interesting because it is so poorly represented in the statistics of sound. The width of the longitudinal vibrations inside an instrument pipe (sound vibrations are all longitudinal) is restricted by the pipe's internal diameter, so that it is not until the full length of the pipe has been traversed, or some form of side opening occurs, that sideways air pressure of the atmosphere is encountered by the vibrations.

Air pressure from the side inhibits the vibrations by heavily damping them out because there is no energy in a sideways (transverse) direction which will overcome the static pressure of the atmosphere.

So the air vibrations are stopped by a side air pressure (in the same way as a violin string is stopped by finger pressure), but not before their longitudinal energy has impinged on the atmosphere beyond this point. The extent of this impingement will be found in technical books as the end-of-tube correction measurement. However, in this manner the vibrations inside a pipe pass energy into the atmosphere and quite naturally the atmospheric pressure reacts with counter vibrations straight back up the pipe. By this action the fundamental frequency becomes compounded, but the compound vibrations reach the pipe opening and their effect is carried through the atmosphere by the reflected vibrations propagated beyond the control of the pipe. The reflected frequencies are therefore free to travel and spread to the extent of their energy.

HARMONICS

In sound and musical studies the word harmonic is used for different references. In the first case as a name for a vibration frequency and in the second case as the single pitch of sound produced by one frequency and called a 'tone', or, because of its singleness, a pure sound. There is also the application of the word in 'harmonic' notes, which is a reference to notes formed from one of the higher harmonic tones in a note, as against the note formed from the lowest one. This subject is explained in later pages. Not all the elements of frequency or sound are called harmonics, those which do not conform to a simple relationship with each other retain only the general description of 'partials'.

The individual frequencies of vibrations each known as an harmonic frequency, occur in a pipe because the air within supports the resonance (reacts in sympathy) of both a full-length vibration for one pitch of sound and to proportionately shorter lengths for other sounds all at the same time. This also gives a slightly modified form of resonance called 'coupled vibration', in stabilising the reed vibrations to an harmonic frequency, which is a very important basis in the 'coupled' system for the complete instrument. (A reed must be capable of true and easy vibration reaction for this adjustment on every note.)

By being of individual frequency, each harmonic has quite a separate identity but is treated as the unit of one single 'tone' (pure sound). A note of pure sound is demonstrated by the single 'tone' sound of a tuning fork which is easily detectable from the same pitch of instrumental note containing a number of 'tone' elements together. Because there are a number of these frequencies together within an instrument pipe, there is a complication of vibrations, but these, acting in only two directions, either conform with or counteract each other with good definition, which gives a strong compound resultant of frequencies for sounding just any one note. Harmonics are thus the frequencies with strong influence in the combination of 'tones' which forms an instrumental note. This may be visualised as 'a tone' of full-length frequency with smaller units of higher frequencies imposed within it and these fit into the combination 'harmoniously'.

The harmonic 'tones' or individual frequencies are numbered for reference purposes, from one upwards, each rising number indicating a rise in the pitch of sound and a rise to a higher frequency. Each subsequent rise is not an equal step in the rise of pitch. The pitch rises proportionately less for each step taken upwards, but any of these elements can be described by its harmonic number and this is commonly used.

The first harmonic element or 'tone' has the lowest frequency and the longest vibrations in a note and this would be shown by the abbreviation H1 but for the fact that it is generally called the fundamental note of the harmonic series. Taking the frequency of any 'tone' as that of a fundamental sound (H1), its next higher harmonic has twice that frequency of vibrations and this (H2) harmonic sounds a note one octave higher than the fundamental H1. The next harmonic has the same amount of frequency increase, but this time the musical increase is not an octave and H3 is only a musical fifth higher than H2. Further harmonics have the same amount of frequency increase, but H4 only reaches a musical fourth, so it sounds the second octave above the fundamental note, then H5, H6 and H7 all come before the sound of the third octave H8, and so on. The ascending harmonics, from a fundamental note of C, are C (H2), G (H3), C (H4), E (H5), G (H6), B flat (H7), C (H8), etc. This first eight of the 'tones' indicates how strong the 'tone' or harmonic-sounding C exists in the note C, followed in intensity by the G's, being two in number. All the strongest harmonics within a note played, say, on a piano can be audibly detected.

The number, selection and relative intensity of harmonic tones depends on the acoustic development by the instrument used to produce the note. Such variations in harmonic content are entirely responsible for the characteristic tonal quality of each kind of instrument and result from the extremely complicated process previously indicated of the mixing and multiple 'phasing' of frequencies which arises from the resonance peculiar to each instrument. A note with prominent high harmonics as that of the clarinet is brighter and more piercing in tone than one which has only the lower range of harmonics evident, giving a sweeter and duller sound, as the tone of the saxophone.

Two other general factors affect the richness of harmonic content as between different instruments. One is the length of the pipe to contain the air column in which the note is generated: with a longer air column, more harmonics will generally be discernible than those in the same note produced by a shorter air column on the same instrument. The other is the audible range available for the production of harmonics. Harmonics range higher in pitch from their fundamental note, so low-voiced instruments have a potential advantage over those covering only higher-sounding notes, because a larger number of harmonics can be generated between the fundamental 'tone' and the upper limit of audibility.

The term 'overtones' refers only to harmonic 'tones' which are higher than the fundamental.

THE SCALE

The present standard or ordinary musical scale of 'equal temperament', as it is called, gives a slight mistuning to all twelve semitone-intervals in an octave. This is arranged to enable keyboard instruments to sound reasonably well in tune when playing in any key of music, and if the mistuning is accurately placed, the key-colour differences are reduced. This makes them unnoticeable to most ears, as the scale has become more or less acceptable through long use.

The term equal temperament apparently indicates that the increase in vibration frequency for each of the twelve semitones in an octave is proportioned in the ratio of one-twelfth of the ratio of increase for the whole octave, which is 1 : 2 (a note's frequency is only half that of its octave higher note). All the other notes within the octave are not equally or evenly tempered to musical intervals but to a recurring mathematical one. The semitone rise is therefore by ratio and the whole tone has 'twice the power' of the semitone calculation, the major third four times and the fifth seven times the power of the semitone calculation and so on.

The change from any note to that of a semitone higher is calculated by multiplying the lower frequency by 1.0595, which figure approximates the 1/12th root of 2 ($2^{1/12}$). This can, however, be simplified into a multiplication factor of 5.95/100, the equivalent of nearly 6 per cent rise in frequency for each individual step of a semitone.

If the note 'A' is 440 Hz, then the note 'A sharp', a semitone higher, will be 440×5.95/100, which results in 466.18 Hz. The ratio of increase for a whole tone becomes 1.0595×1.0595, which equals 1.1225 times, so that if the note C is 261.63 Hz, then note D a tone higher is 261.63×1.1225, that is 293.68 Hz. But practically all the notes tuned to the ratio are not precisely true and are in varying degree rendered flat or sharp in pitch, so that even piano tuners are known to use slight personal deviations.

It is a fact that only the octaves of this musical scale are intended to be precisely in tune. Of the first eight harmonic notes listed in the previous section (harmonically these can be taken from any note) the scale of equal temperament ratio makes four of these exactly in tune because they are octave notes, but the higher the other notes are from the lowest sounding one, the greater is the effect of frequency discrepancy between them. As stated earlier, the above ratio is used for the convenience of tuning keyboard instruments, and when one of these is not included in the playing ensemble, it will be found that the relationship of frequencies is apt to follow the natural proportions of scale progressions. For the major scale of eight notes, the frequency proportions then developed may progress from 1 to $1\frac{1}{8}$, $1\frac{1}{4}$, $1\frac{1}{3}$, $1\frac{1}{2}$, $1\frac{2}{3}$, $1\frac{7}{8}$, and 2 (octave). Either because of or in spite of these scale arrangements, players will find that flexibility of frequency on every note of the clarinet and saxophone instruments is essential to maintain comfortable intonation in varying ensembles. An orchestra not including a piano or similar keyboard instrument does not play strictly to the scale of equal temperament as a rule and intervals between notes may be taken either 'wider' or 'narrower' according to melodic or harmonic considerations and for the tone quality of the notes to improve concordance.

So long as the above principles are understood and frequency adjustment becomes a habit involving constant listening to the music being played, the actual frequency figures as developed for the scale need not be pursued.

1

The clarinet principle. Materials and their characteristics. Choice of various instruments. Tuning new instruments.

The sound-producing principle in single-reed wind instruments and in the reed-pipes of an organ is the same. The sound produced is markedly similar even though the resonator pipes of the organ are much simpler. To understand the principle, it is therefore helpful to consider first the layout of an organ reed-pipe.

For sounding the same voice as the clarinet, an organ reed-pipe is in the same form and this is known as a stopped pipe. At one end it has an enclosure called a boot and this contains a slightly curved tongue of metal as a reed, arranged to vibrate over a slot cut through a flat surface formed on a tube and thus resembling a mouthpiece. Each organ-pipe produces only one note and the pitch of this note is governed by the length of reed and by the length of the resonator pipe, each being tuned for only that note. For this reason every note has a separate complete pipe and these vary in length between a few inches for the highest notes and a few feet for the lowest. Reed-tuning is provided by a control wire positioned across the reed as a bar, which will adjust the length of reed free to vibrate.

Compared with this relatively straightforward organ reed-pipe, other wind-instrument reed-pipes have become extremely complex, thereby producing a great range of notes. This is achieved by the multi-tuning of a single reed-pipe. The clarinet and saxophone are both basically reed-pipe instruments, although the clarinet pipe has a generally parallel bore, while the saxophone has a conical bore. The conical bore has an increase in diameter of about 1 in 18 and this is quite simple to check on the alto saxophone instrument. The outside tube diameter will be found to

10

be about 1 inch just below the crook socket and 2 inches just above the bottom bend 18 inches further down the instrument. Both instruments are fitted with the familiar open and stopped holes to provide for the different notes and registers to be produced through the one pipe. The

Fig. 1. **Organ reed pipe**

1 Pipe (resonator). *The size and style are varied by makers' unending ingenuity and art, for producing the pitch and quality of notes.*

2 Block. *This basic component is externally shaped for fitting the boot (airtight cover) with blowing hole in its cone-shaped tip (not shown).*

3 Tuning wire (spring). *Passing through the block, the wire provides external adjustment for matching the reed's length of vibrating tip to the pipe's pitch and tone of note.*

4 Slot (flue, or in German, schlot). *This is cut at the closed end of a hollow stalk, in German, a schlotte. In English these are both commonly misnamed shallot. A slightly parabolic-curved metal tongue or reed (not shown) is held over the slot by a wedge.*

function of the tuning wire is performed by the player's lips. The lips can be reinforced at will by using the teeth as 'backing' when controlling the pressure on the reed. As the reed operates inside the mouth a personal tone element exists which is quite distinct from the embouchure in relation to the control of the reed. Moreover, on the clarinet and saxophone the reed is frequently removed and changed, also each reed has its own peculiar complex and variable nature, which may produce differences in sound according to variations in the reed grain or in the overall thickness of its wedge-shaped form, with one flat side and the other curved, or in the amount of absorbed and external moisture present in its working conditions. In spite of all these contrasts, the clarinet and its organ counterpart produce sounds of comparable quality. Because it is a stopped-pipe instrument, the clarinet 'speaks' or overblows in twelfths instead of in octaves as on the saxophone and other reed instruments, so the use of harmonic notes on the clarinet involves this interval, unlike any other instrument.

MATERIALS AND THEIR CHARACTERISTICS

Wooden clarinets are now generally made from an almost black wood classified under various names: black cocus, ebony, grenadilla and others. Disadvantages of wood include the possibility of cracking as it becomes alternately wet and dry in use, and a liability to variation in accuracy of instrument tuning owing to minute changes in the wood itself. Even a normally well-fitting instrument is affected after more than a week or two of everyday playing sessions, owing to the swelling and shrinking of the wood. An early sign of the effect of breath-moisture on the wood is that one of the joints, most often that between the barrel and the upper part of the instrument, becomes abnormally tight-fitting. It may be impossible—or at least unwise to try—to refit these parts together or even part them, because forcible handling can cause keywork damage. Even the best-quality instruments, made from wood which is reputed to be fully and properly seasoned, cannot be expected to be immune to this reaction. Conversely, a wooden instrument which is left for several weeks without being played may be found to have loose joints. Hot water applied to the cork inserts of the joints will make them swell immediately and the instrument will be usable once more.

Small tone-holes are also liable to be affected by the moisture sufficiently to vary the tuning of notes, and endeavours to correct this by embouchure adjustment or other means during playing can lead to irritating changes of tone or technique.

If the development of the conditions produced by moisture is left unchecked this may even cause the keywork to require re-adjustment and, in extreme cases, may result in the wood actually cracking or splitting. To reduce this all too common trouble caused by alternate moisture and dryness in instruments, the bore should be served with olive oil or raw linseed oil to fill up the grain of the wood and replace moisture in dried-out areas. If this is done several times, cracks should not develop. Too much linseed oil may, however, form a skin, so any surplus should be removed. If small tone-holes are left with a thick lining of oil, a skin which forms from the oil will reduce their size and affect the tuning of the notes they control. Oil must also be kept off the pads by covering them during the oiling process.

To eliminate the disadvantages of wood, ebonite is also used for making clarinets. The tone of ebonite instruments is good, much like that of wooden ones. A slight difference in the resonance of the materials can be detected by some players, but most listeners are unaware of it. Discoloration by heat or strong light may occur but can be polished out of ebonite: the material's solid texture seems to give a more general expansion and contraction movement than wood by temperature changes, which has been found to be less detrimental to the tuning of an ebonite instrument. However, where keywork is already loose, expansion in conditions of heat can give trouble by causing extra keywork play, so that a pad can come down upon its tone-hole out of true and it does not then seat properly. Alternatively, in cold conditions, contraction has been known to make close-fitting keywork stiff in action.

The advent of resin-fibre and plastics has had its own effect on reed instruments. It is too early to know how much better than ebonite these materials may become, but great improvements of accuracy in manufacture at reduced cost should be possible.

Finally there are metal clarinets. These have not been popular because the tone has been noticeably dissimilar to that of wooden instruments and changes of temperature have acutely affected the pitch level of notes. Flutes recently made of light metal with the thickness of wood are proving satisfactory, but so too have previous metal flutes. The flute is so different from the clarinet, however, that it must not automatically be assumed that similar developments will immediately ensue in the manufacture of clarinets.

The mouthpiece fitted on single-reed instruments has virtually come to be considered as a separate item from the rest of the instrument, owing to many years of experiment by players and others to create changes of tone or a better combination of sound generator (mouthpiece) and resonator (pipe) in the instrument, by using a different mouthpiece. Instead of a mouthpiece being individually matched to each instrument, a large selection of mouthpieces is now produced to go with all the popular instruments. For making a choice from these, information on makers' ranges and mouthpiece classification marks is included in a section of Chapter 4.

CHOICE OF CLARINETS

By far the most popular instrument is the B flat soprano. For classical works and some lighter music this has to be augmented by the closely pitched model in A, for which much important music is written. The development of separate instruments, with a difference of a mere semitone in pitch, originated from fingering and tuning difficulties on early forms of the instrument when playing in remote keys of music. The B flat instrument was used for its own and other flat keys, but for playing with orchestral strings, frequently in a key of three or more sharps, the clarinet in A had, and still has, the advantage of simplicity of fingering for these keys. The two instruments have the same bore and the same mouthpiece, barrel and bell. On the B flat, however, the keywork is set higher up the instrument towards the mouthpiece and is a little more closely spaced, so that for the same fingering it plays a semitone higher than the A instrument. On account of the higher keywork position, the B flat instrument length is also fractionally shorter than that of the A instrument.

The B flat instrument is also made in a longer model which adds an extra semitone at the lower end of its range: it is then the same length as the A instrument and is able to produce the same lowest-sounding note. The extra key which plays this note, written low E flat, also gives the overblown B flat a twelfth above—which is a most useful alternative fingering for the B flat note in the throat register (see Figure 17). Because the length and bore of the two instruments are exactly the same, these notes, E flat and B flat, sound precisely the same as the low E and the middle B notes of the A clarinet.

Although less frequently required by players, there is a variant of the A clarinet which has a key for playing its low E flat and middle B flat notes, a practice which is followed for the lowest notes on all the lower-voiced instruments. Some bass clarinets are made with an extended range down to low C.

The C soprano clarinet is smaller than the A and B flat instruments and has a noticeably shriller tone. This is sufficient reason for using it in suitable circumstances. Very little orchestral music is written for the C clarinet, much less than for the A: but what there is has often to be played by the B flat and A player, who is then faced with playing music for all three instruments. Music for the C clarinet is therefore mostly transposed by the player and played on the B flat instrument (see *Transposing*, Chapter 7). Only in special circumstances is the extra expense of providing and maintaining a C clarinet justified.

Many orchestral players equip themselves with 'a pair of clarinets', which means one A and one B flat instrument, in order to follow the purpose of their original use, which is to allow the clarinet to flourish in the musical keys written for each one. If music for the A instrument is not frequently played, the instrument should still be used for practice periods to avoid wearing out the B flat clarinet pads and keywork. Clarinet players using only the B flat instrument may at some time encounter saxophone music and they can then consider using one of the saxophones as a second instrument. For saxophone players a similar situation can occur in reverse.

OTHER CLARINETS

The clarinet family includes instruments of many other sizes and pitches: some are obsolete, while others are only used for a few older musical works requiring them. After the sopranos, the next most useful instrument is the baritone/bass in B flat; then for larger ensembles comes the choice of the high-pitched E flat sopranino. The alto/tenor in E flat and the basset-horn in F have only limited use. All these, with other models in higher, intermediate and lower pitches, are readily obtainable from the instrument makers.

In this book the soprano clarinet with the Boehm system of keywork and fingering is the subject of reference except where otherwise indicated.

CHOICE OF SAXOPHONES

Although saxophones may appear to be less exacting instruments than clarinets, much that is written for the clarinet in this book can in principle be applied to the saxophone. When the saxophone is chosen as a primary instrument, the popular choice is for either the alto or the tenor model. Both these instruments have important solo roles included in their music, and expertise can be rewarding as well as satisfying. For a second instrument, other than adding a saxophone of different pitch, the B flat clarinet has already been mentioned, and the flute is at present a great favourite owing to the similarity of its fingering to that of the saxophone. The tenor or baritone saxophone player can add the bass/baritone clarinet to his choice.

As a separate section or with clarinets, saxophones are much used in military bands, recording groups, dance bands, theatre and light orchestras, but they appear in symphony orchestras only on the infrequent occasions when musical works are played which specifically require the inclusion of the saxophone sound (see *Tone*, Chapter 6). Four saxophones can be used together to good effect and quartet music for sweet-toned performance could be more popular.

The family of saxophones includes the C (natural) and B flat sopranos, the latter in straight and curved shapes: the E flat alto: the C (natural) and B flat tenors: the E flat baritone and the B flat bass. The E flat alto saxophone takes the lead in most forms of saxophone section, except in especially arranged quartets. The B flat tenor is a popular solo instrument and usually gives an even voice throughout its full range for the minimum of effort. The E flat baritone has a low solo voice and can be used also as a flexible bass for any ensemble. The convenience or awkwardness of size—even more critical than weight in some cases—might affect a choice of one of these instruments.

The B flat soprano saxophone is often used for the high voice in saxophone concert quartets. Its tone can be superb, but it has not attained universal popularity owing to a reputation for difficulties in achieving impeccable intonation. Such notoriety may well stem from a player's incapacity to control the short conical bore which demands critical pitching from the embouchure to maintain balance in tuning. If the clarinet and the soprano saxophone are used alternately, as when doubling in one musical work, the changes of instrument will be found more exacting than would be the case in changing between instruments of different voices or larger members of the families.

The tarogato is a hybrid instrument in the shape of a soprano saxophone, but it is built in wood. It is a Hungarian folk instrument, the orchestral use of which appears to be limited to that of providing the characteristic music of a shepherd's pipe.

The saxophone instrument is limited in range compared with the clarinet: in fact the B flat clarinet is sometimes used for the highest voice

Table 1. Saxophone high-note fingering

Note	F♯	F♯	F♯	G	G	G	G	G♯	G♯	G♯	A	A	A	A	B♭	B♭	B♭	B♭	B	B	C	C	C♯	C♯	D
Palm keys														D	E♭	E♭	E♭	E♭ / D	E♭?	E♭	E♭ / D	F	E♭ / D	F / D	F / E♭ / D
									Octave key open in each case																
Left-hand plates *(Top F plate)*	–	O	–	–	O	–	–	–	O	–	O	–	–	–	O	O	–	–	O	O	–	O	–	O	O
	O	O	O	–	O	O	–	–	O	–	–	–	–	O	O	O	O	–	O	O	O	O	O	O	O
	–	–	O	–	–	O	–	–	–	–	–	–	O	–	–	–	–	O	–	O	O	O	O	O	O
Side keys	1			2	1	2		2	2	2	2		2		2				3?	3				3	3
																			2						
Right-hand plates *(F♯ key)*	–	–	O?	–	O	O	–	–	O	O	O	O	–	O	–	O	–	O	–	–	–	O	–	O	O
	–	O	O	O	O	–	O	O	O	O	–	O	O	–	O	–	O	–	O	O	O	O	O	O	O
	O	–	–	O	–	–	O	–	O	–	O	–	–	–	O	–	O	–	O	–	O	–	O	–	O
Low keys	B♭ / E♭			E♭ / E♭			E♭ / E♭		E♭ / E♭		E♭	E♭			E♭ / E♭										

Symbols used in fingering tables

O indicates open finger-hole or finger-plate.
– indicates closed finger-hole or finger-plate.
Ө or ? indicates optional use.
1 to 4 indicates side key to use.
Other keys are marked by their notation letters.

in a section of four or more saxophones, taking advantage of the greater range and disregarding the difference in tone. The range of two and a half octaves for saxophones is from written B flat below, to F above the stave. A few instruments are made with extra keys to extend this from A below to F sharp above, but these are not always available. Harmonic notes will increase the range upwards by a sixth to high D, but fingering for these notes is complex, so that their use is limited to long-sounding notes used as 'bell' notes.

The saxophone speaks in octaves (eighths), so the tuning by embouchure of the harmonic notes is simpler than the twelfths of the clarinet. On notes sounded by a short length of the instrument, the saxophone tuning requires a careful embouchure to give sweet tone production. Particularly on the soprano instrument, an unsuitable embouchure will produce indifferent results.

Saxophones which have been stripped of silver or other plating, and re-finished in lacquered brass to fulfil a change in fashion, should be avoided unless they are personally proved to be satisfactory. The processing and re-polishing usually results in an unsatisfactory condition in such instruments. Identification of these instruments is made possible by slight traces of plating found in inaccessible corners, under springs, pads or cork stops. Silver or other metal-plated instruments are preferable to those with a lacquered brass finish, if only for the cleaner interior and the more permanent exterior appearance of saxophones which plating provides.

INSTRUMENT CASES

Instrument cases are often sold separately, being the products of a case rather than an instrument maker. Cases are made for personal carrying. If an instrument has to be sent on a journey, it should be packed with extra cushioning inside the case, to prevent movement which might bend the keys. Most clarinet cases have insufficient room for accessories if the list includes an alternative barrel or an extra mouthpiece. Other items which might be housed in a case are a pull-through, a polishing duster, a box of reeds, a reed cutter and scraping knife, a screw-driver, a tuning fork or pitch pipe, adhesive tape for music, a pencil and indiarubber, blotting paper for wet pads, an oil bottle or can, joint grease, the player's spectacles and a compartment to house an instrument stand or pegs. The list of necessities indicates that the size of case generally supplied to hold two clarinets might well be used to hold one and accessories. Tall, thin cases fall over at a slight touch: placed flat they may be trodden on, or used as a resting-place for anything by anyone. Locks and handles should be silent in operation, as an enclosed instrument or an accessory will be urgently required during a hushed performance sooner or later. Even a slight disturbance at such a time constitutes a major misdemeanour which it is well worth while to avoid.

TUNING NEW INSTRUMENTS

Instruments produced in a factory are not tuned to the degree required by most players. Testing carried out using a factory tester's mouthpiece is unlikely to be matched by a purchaser using any mouthpiece of choice and also perhaps another barrel. Cheaper and more expensive instruments are alike in this respect: they should have additional note-tuning. The aim of this should be to ensure that the embouchure has to make as little adjustment as possible to correct any note, because undue embouchure variation is a handicap to playing technique. A note sounding sharp will cause a pitch-conscious player to relax the embouchure in adjustment of the pitch, and the loss of reed control thus suffered can result in a squeak. On the other hand, a note sounding flat requires correction by an undue tightening of the embouchure. Both these conditions involve a deterioration in tone.

A clarinet needs to be played for several weeks at least, before the wood is settled to playing condition and the instrument is ready for testing the tuning between notes. After that, final tuning is a long process to be carried out over a period of regular playing in all registers and musical keys. During this gradual process, the tuning of all the notes controlled by each tone-hole must be carefully considered as a group, including those notes produced by alternative fingerings. Pads are of course abnormally dry on new instruments and are liable to take altered seatings with use and moisture. The clearance of pads from tone-holes is critical and these can be checked as later explained. At present it should be noted that the correct clearance of pads from the tone-holes is not the same for all keys on the instrument.

On the clarinet the tuning between the low E and the middle B notes —the long twelfth as it is called—is seldom perfect. When the instrument is 'cold' (not warmed up by playing) the middle B note should in fact sound noticeably below pitch and this may make the low E note sound sharp in comparison. At the other end of the instrument, the throat register note B flat will also be flat in pitch, but the alternative side-key fingering should not sound quite so flat, even on a cold instrument (see *Barrel*, Chapter 3, and *Tuning*, Chapter 6). Faults in tuning can sometimes be detected by playing notes quickly in octaves and also in fifths, up and down. This action helps to show up any discrepancy in the tuning, in the first moment that a note sounds, before an embouchure change has time to correct it. Duplicate fingerings can be checked against each other and other intervals right down to semitones are tuned in the course of time.

Only after this, and playing a clarinet in an ensemble of other instruments, can the balance of the tuning be finally adjudged and fully appreciated. All the above tuning items are more fully dealt with under separate headings in later chapters.

2

Keywork: the metal. Boehm clarinet variations. Adjustment of touchpieces and springs. Possible improvements. Saxophone adjustments.

KEYWORK METAL

Most clarinet keywork is made of nickel silver, sometimes called German silver or by its French name maillechort. The metal is cut and hammered into shape. There was a different metal and method which was only a little used and this is mentioned under 'adjustments'. Nickel silver varies in nickel content, but it has more than 15 per cent if the quality is good, and this makes it a white nickel-brass. Owing to the softness of the metal, keywork may wear quickly; but on the whole it is tough, ductile, white in colour and easily cleaned so that it does not really need to be plated for the sake of appearance. In spite of this, most instruments are currently supplied with plated keywork and a choice of the plating is often available.

Although plating is mostly added for improved appearance, it also adds strength to the soft metal keywork. Chromium plating is so thick and hard that it will crack and peel off the keys if they become bent. The polished finish of the plating makes the touchpieces slippery and a fingernail-end touch on a key means a certain slip just as much as do perspiring fingers. Touchpieces can be roughened by rubbing them with emery paper to provide a better finger grip, though naturally this will be rather detrimental to the instrument's appearance.

BOEHM CLARINET VARIATIONS

Few players make any change from the type of keywork used during their student days, because this means learning again to use some different keywork arrangement. Many doubtless consider that any temporary disturbance of their hard-won technique is not justified, so they 'make do' with whatever instrument they already use. As an example of this, there are some players still using instruments with less keywork than that of the plain Boehm, because they have become so well accustomed to their instruments through years of playing. When really serious study and unrestricted performance is contemplated the great advantages to be gained from making a wise choice of instrument are extremely important.

The plain, ordinary or standard model Boehm clarinet is supplied by most manufacturers in several qualities at a great variance of price. The keywork is quoted as being of seventeen keys and six rings (including the one at the back around the thumb-hole). This is the basic and most popular model in general use, widely adopted as standard at colleges and conservatoires.

Further models with improved and additional keywork are available to include one or more of the following improvements in this sequence. First, an extra ring for use by the third finger of the left hand, to provide a forked fingering for E flat/B flat and high F notes. Second, an articulated mechanism for the fourth-finger left-hand C sharp/G sharp key (as provided in this position on all saxophones). A clarinet with this addition to the key has the appropriate tone-hole position moved from the underside of the instrument to the top side (front), where the hole is placed in line with the row of finger-holes. With this arrangement the common nuisance of 'water blobs in the G sharp key' is eliminated. Third, an extra lever with touchpiece, again for the left hand fourth finger, which duplicates the operation of the right G sharp/D sharp key. This lever completes the (left and right hand) duplication for all fourth-finger touchpieces, and this is an asset for constant use by players 'reading' music in sharp keys. Finally, there is the full or fully improved model Boehm clarinet which includes all these keywork additions and also is extended in length to increase its playing range by a semitone to low E flat. An extra key for this note is grouped with the others operated by the right-hand fourth finger (see Plate 1). This key also provides the additional benefit of an excellent clarion register B flat note and has also proved convenient for playing A sharp/C sharp shakes.

The superior range of keywork obviously makes this a more expensive clarinet, especially as it is fitted on better-quality instruments. The im-

When possible,put note groups in the same register.

The low E♭ key,(used for B♭) avoids left hand awkwardness.

Example 1

proved instrument, however, does make easier playing possible, which may be more particularly appreciated by players who perform a wide variety of music rather than those who have a more restricted repertoire. The full Boehm keywork should also be favourably considered by musicians who play two instruments of which one is the clarinet, because of the avoidance of extra 'cross' and fake fingerings. Otherwise these have to be remembered for playing in remote keys of music. As noted above, the player has an immediate and free choice of using either hand for fourth-finger keys, which is easier as well as being more efficient than the bugbear of the set, and sometimes awkward, sequences of fingering which otherwise occur.

Users of the ordinary model instrument may still from time to time endeavour to justify their choice by questioning the desirability or necessity of the extra keywork, but such opinions not substantiated by a regular use of the better instrument can be safely disregarded, and must not be allowed to mislead players who would choose the best for themselves. Obviously all the older works of music had originally to be played on much less perfect keywork than that found on any present-day instrument, but it is a fact that musical requirements for sound studio standards continue to make ever-increasing demands, and the technical development of clarinet design has failed to advance at the same pace. As a result, neither the standard nor even the full Boehm keywork can be considered to be truly up to date mechanically, any more than can most other small fittings made to designs of long standing.

There are other points to watch in making a choice of instrument, which apply not so much to one model of keywork as against another, but to details of the general standard of manufacture. Keywork pivoted on point screws gives a light and quickly responsive action, but the pivot points are apt to wear slack. Play in instrument keywork causes pads to move on tone-holes, which besides displacing the set positions, wears pads excessively on the tone-hole edges. Screws with a 'finger' extension rather than just a point on them are a much improved pivot. Keys with through rods as an alternative to pivot screws require stronger springing to overcome the greater friction of the rods, particularly if keys become slightly bent. Careful lubrication is needed if these keys are not to be sluggish in operation (molybdenum disulphide may be preferred to oil lubrication).

The rings around the finger-holes should be exactly level with the tops of the holes when the fingers press the rings down. An offset position of the tone-hole for the left-hand third finger is very helpful in allowing the fourth finger to reach its levers easily without danger of disturbing the third finger's position. In the pressed position, the height of fourth-finger right-hand keys for E flat and C, situated over the C sharp and B keys, must be sufficient for good finger clearance over the latter. Notice also that the angle made by this complete group of touchpieces with the line of the instrument body varies between instruments.

In these and other small details, keywork varies in fingering positions and this gives a different 'feel' between one make of instrument and another, also between models of the same make. A shape and position of keywork really well suited to the player's hands are vital for successful relaxed performance, and a personal search for the most acceptable key-work arrangement should be diligently pursued. Covered hole or 'à plateaux' clarinets dispense with open finger-holes and rings, in place of which are solid pad cups with pads fitted, which make the appearance of this part of the keywork comparable with that of the flute or the bass clarinet.

Although the long-established Boehm system of keywork is the one most generally used on clarinets and is exclusively used on saxophones, other more recently developed variations for the clarinet are the Oehler and what has become known as the Schmidt Reform Boehm. The latter is a large-bore instrument (see *Bore*, Chapter 3) and both have the tone-holes more evenly spaced along the instrument.

KEYWORK ADJUSTMENTS

To supplement the best choice of keywork, minor adjustments can be made to the keys to cater for personal needs, but these must be carried out with expert care and restraint to avoid expensive mistakes. It is essential to ascertain the composition of the keywork beforehand, as a few instruments have been made with cast metal keys which are inevitably quite brittle and the touchpieces cannot therefore be re-positioned. Even if the keywork on such an instrument happens to fit the player's hands, it is undesirable to have keywork which fractures rather too easily. Apart from this cast metal keywork, many keys can be adjusted a little to accommodate the player.

Awkward keywork will cause the player's fingers to get out of position on the instrument keys, and this keywork can be detected during repetitions of a difficult passage or phrase of music, if played at speed. Quick changes from one instrument to another which involve the use of slightly dissimilar keywork, even the difference of key spacing as between the B flat and the A clarinets, will also bring misjudgement of finger positions, so it is wise to do everything possible to minimise any loss of control.

The difficulty of returning out-of-place fingers to their positions is often overcome by the feel of the key springing, so that adding or relieving the tension of keywork springs to the following pattern of recommendations should help to remedy some of these fingering difficulties. Spring adjustment, however, may be a difficult and delicate job, so before altering the spring itself it is worth while getting some idea of the effect of a change in tension by tying a rubber band over or under a key and anchored under tension to another part of the keywork, although the control of this form of tension is so haphazard that it must only be considered a very rough guide.

Springing needs to be strong enough to return a key without it bouncing, or fast notes will be affected; also to enable the player to feel the location of a key without moving it. Transverse keys, like the right-hand middle-finger one, need firm springing to avoid the pads being eased off the tone-holes accidentally, by the side of the finger rubbing or pressing the key sideways while it is out of use between the fingers. Closed keys should have stronger springing than open keys; the latter need only be sprung strong enough for trill note speed with the instrument held in the playing position. Keys with actions which require pressing on to the side of an instrument rather than on the front or vertical should be sprung as lightly as possible to eliminate the danger of the spring resistance causing the instrument to be pushed to one side when they are used. In cases where one touchpiece controls two keys, the lower action can be given slightly stronger springing to make the keys work as one.

Clarinet and saxophone springs are adjusted by bending or resetting them to increase or decrease the tension. To do this a very small pair of smooth flat-nosed pliers, say about four inches long, are necessary. Needle spring steel is hard and brittle, but shaped springs are softened and flattened at the thick end where they fit through the pillar. It is only this part of the spring which can be bent, because the softness has made it less brittle. Springs already fitted on an instrument can be altered by holding them in the centre with the pliers, which are then twisted carefully to *slightly* alter the direction in which the spring points. If a spring is just pushed to one side the pillar may turn in the instrument, and the spring will go round with it without being re-set. A very small spring may need 'straightening' by as little as one millimetre in the position of the spring's point, to reduce the tension, or about two millimetres point-alteration of 'increased curve' when increasing the tension—and a little more for larger springs.

If a spring will not hold its tension, it may be too soft and should be replaced by a new one. To remove a spring or a broken one, the point end is pushed all the way back through the spring-hole in the pillar. Only a new spring of the same thickness will fit the hole and the spring should also be measured for length to suit the key, then fitted to curve in the same direction as the previous spring. To secure the spring, the flattened end is jammed in the pillar by forcing these together between the pliers.

Thumb locations in relation to touchpiece positions are especially important, because adjustment of these can prove to be so beneficial for so many players. The left-hand thumb has to operate the speaker key and open or seal the thumb-hole in every possible sequence. The speaker key is usually positioned so that it almost touches the thumb-hole ring; but the acceptable proximity here ought to be decided by the size and shape of the player's thumb. The speaker key may therefore require shortening if it touches the thumb when the thumb is in the natural central position for covering the hole. A speaker or other key must first be removed from the instrument before filing a small flat on the end of the touchpiece to shorten it by the estimated amount and when the new length is established the original rounded shape can be remade to restore normal appearance.

When the right-hand thumb rest is not in the best position, any of the fourth finger keys may be difficult to use. The thumb rest is often too low on the instrument to allow the particularly important access to the C sharp key, in which cases the rest should be raised to a position from which this strongly sprung key is within straight-finger reach (see Plate 1). The reason for this is that opening the C sharp key also works the

Plate 1. **Fourth-finger position**

C key and so the fourth finger has to press against two springs. No note sounds until the C key is fully closed, so although the C sharp key must have a strong spring for closing, comparatively light springing and a careful choice between left and right hand fingering are essential for the fast working of the C sharp key.

In addition to the thumb rest position, the right-hand fourth-finger touchpieces may be reshaped to accommodate the length and width of

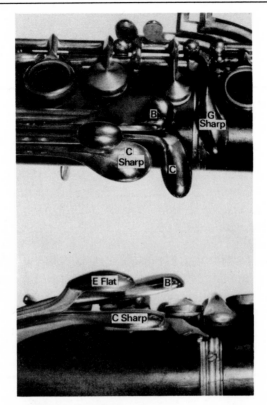

Part A

Part B

Plate 2. Touchpiece layout

Part A. *For unhindered fingering, the distance between the G sharp, C, C sharp and B keys must allow generous finger-width clearance.*

Part B. *A level position for all these touchpieces, at near tone-hole-top elevation, simplifies fourth-finger action. Note the G sharp and C note touchpieces particularly. The raised level of B note touchpiece must give ample finger-action clearance in addition to key clearance from the C sharp key.*

the finger. The B and C sharp touchpieces must be well spaced and shaped so that the finger does not obstruct the return of the right-hand C sharp touchpiece, after this note has been played left-handed and is followed by note B right-handed. For the finger to pass naturally to the B and C sharp touchpieces without pulling the third finger from its hole-covering position, the C and E flat touchpieces above them may be seen to be too long, in which case the ends can be filed as outlined in a previous paragraph (see Plate 1). The E flat touchpiece should come to rest in a position just lower than that for the C key, so that even if the finger sags, it clears the E flat key absolutely when the C key is being held down tightly.

Fourth-finger keys do not open their respective vents by the same distance. The distances, controlled by the leverage differences of the keys and the limited movement of the 'swallow tail' coupling from the C key touchpiece, are permanently set for the correct tuning of the notes from the appropriate tone-holes. When fitting new pads or making any adjustments, these conditions must be retained.

The left-hand fourth-finger G sharp key and the long C key touchpieces are sometimes wrapped around the instrument body where they are difficult to use. They must stand off the instrument and be turned for the finger to work at the same angle as that for the other fingers (see Plate 2). If the B and C sharp long levers are thin, they may be weak. Their action may be springy and cause slow speaking. The B lever can be well tested by playing a B to D shake, for which the pads must seal nicely. Releasing these keys is usually a slower operation than pressing them.

The left-hand first-finger keys for G sharp and A must open exactly together when playing the A note. The adjusting screw, if fitted, should be regularly inspected and if necessary reset so that no fuzzy note sounds before the second key opens. A cork insert between the keys instead of a screw is preferable to an unreliable or loose screw setting. The speaker and the A keys must also be closely matched in springing so that they open together when pressed simultaneously to play B flat.

When fingers cover the holes on the clarinet they must be *well* clear of the adjacent keys. The first finger must not lie close to the G sharp or the A touchpieces. Without sufficient clearance the finger may occasionally come down on a key, either opening it or the finger being deflected from its objective of the centre of the open hole. If the finger is even momentarily displaced, this delays the next note, which will cause further confusion.

The small transverse keys across the line of the tone-holes, used for B flat and F sharp, must be at the appropriate angle for lying in line with, and be evenly spaced between, the fingers. Adjust these keys if they touch a finger closing a tone-hole. The touchpieces should be kept well up from the instrument, their width might need reducing, and the best positions for them can be observed by playing the instrument before a mirror.

Add cork underneath the lever on the thumb ring (which also controls the first finger ring and small pad), to set the pad as close to the tone-hole as a clear note G (open instrument) will allow. All the other rings and the pads that they control can be similarly adjusted, on the lower lever at the middle joint of the instrument. Check the effect on notes played in the top half of the instrument, by placing a piece of sheet cork under the lever. Whilst playing each note in turn, remove the cork to test whether its additional thickness causes any detriment to note tuning or clarity (see Plate 3).

Instruments with the C sharp/G sharp vent passing through the middle joint may scrape joint grease into the tone-hole when the instrument is assembled. The hole must be kept clear of this or other obstruction, to avoid a flattened note.

POSSIBLE IMPROVEMENTS

Improvement of clarinet keywork is long overdue. Some of the keys fitted at present wear quickly owing to poor mechanical standard and design. The leverage of touchpieces varies too much and the oblique movement given to some keys is most undesirable. The thumb rest underneath the instrument should be adjustable; at present it must be re-positioned if a player has difficulty in working the right-hand fourth-finger keys. The rest is frequently too far down the instrument and may need moving half an inch or even more in extreme cases.

Key touchpieces could be made flat or slightly hollowed so that fingers will rest on them instead of slipping off as the present shape allows. Plating on these parts only increases their unsuitability. Keywork is shaped and fitted unnecessarily close in places, leaving insufficient clearance for expansion, wear and adjustment.

The lowest side key, used by the right-hand first finger for several notes and shakes, has a leverage action in reverse proportions to that for any other key on the clarinet instrument. This means that the finger has to make excessive movement to open and close the key, which is an absurd feature for such a key. On all four of the side keys the fingering action and the venting action are generally oblique. This causes the keys to rub on each other in use if there is any play in the hinge pins. The keys ought to be arranged so that no rubbing can occur even with the most adverse handling, otherwise a key is likely to lift its neighbour

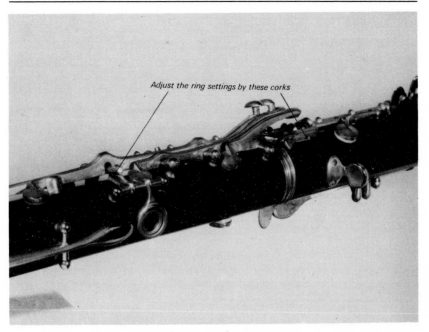

Plate 3. Cork stops

momentarily when opening, or to be sluggish in returning to its closed position.

The shape of clarinet pad-cups allows a popular style of pad with only a small backing card to easily tip or slide out of level when being fitted. A flat seat for a pad in a pad cup as provided on flutes and saxophones gives greater certainty of proper pad support and alignment.

Because twisted pillars (key-posts) trap keys endwise and cause stiff key action, all clarinet pillars carrying springs should have screw-anchored feet locking their position, or the alternative of several pillars mounted together on metal strips or plates, so that there is no chance of a pillar being turned by spring tension or during adjustment. A few anchored posts are fitted on some instruments but these do not fully satisfy keywork requirements.

Fingers are not the best pads for an instrument; they are not flat enough. Variation in the size and shape of players' hands and fingers makes the sealing of tone-holes a considerable hazard for some. The covered hole or 'à plateaux' instrument gives better uniformity of tone-hole covering than the mixed system of finger-holes and pad-covered holes, but few instrument makers at present face the responsibility of producing them efficiently. The bass clarinet is a tribute to the agility of the covered-hole system of keys. On the soprano instruments at present made with open holes and rings—called ring keys in some specifications —some personal problems would be eased by the provision of a padded key for covering the thumb-hole.

Fig. 2. Saxophone mouthpipe cork

Cork sheet 38× 63½ mm (1½× 2½ inches). Shape the sides as shaded and chamfer one end for the underlap. The concave side fits around the rim of the mouthpipe.

SAXOPHONE MOUTHPIPE CORK

A mouthpipe cork cut from a sheet, the same as the clarinet-joint corks, will long outlast the tubular type. Most instrument shops sell sheet cork, the $\frac{1}{32}$ inch thickness of which is usually sufficient for fitting on an alto saxophone mouthpiece and is formed from a rectangular piece $38 \times 63\frac{1}{2}$ mm (see Figure 2). An old razor blade can be used to cut off the black surround strips, leaving one long edge concave and the other convex, with the ends tapered, all of which ensures a nice fit for the taper of the pipe. At one end of this shaped sheet make a 'feathered edge' as marked by the dotted line, thinning with glasspaper the end 6/7 mm, $\frac{1}{4}$ inch, to a slope which forms the underlap and is the first edge to glue to the pipe. Shellac paste or similar waterproof glue must be used for fastening the cork to the pipe, and the *surplus* overlap should not be served with glue or be cut off when fitting. The cork is wrapped tightly around the pipe and bound all over with string to hold it in place until the glue sets. After the string is removed the surplus cork overlap can be trimmed off with a razor blade or very sharp knife. Fine glasspaper will reduce the cut edge along the joint in the cork and produce a good tubular surface with a smooth finish. The mouthpiece must fit firm and airtight along most of the cork's length to accommodate tuning positions. Joint grease will slacken the fit considerably and its use for the protection of the cork against condensation needs to be constantly maintained (see *Condensation*, Chapter 7). A reward of a great many years of easy tuning-up, mouthpiece fitting and adjustment makes this re-corking job well worth while. The mouthpipe fitting to the instrument must likewise be good and airtight; any small leak at these joints will at least cause hard blowing and a loss of tone.

SAXOPHONE KEYWORK ADJUSTMENTS

Straightforward mechanism which allows adjustments to be made to individual keys is better than the extra couplings which are fitted on some instruments and restrict the scope of adjustments. The couplings between the left-hand fourth-finger keys, which are found on saxophones, are difficult to keep in adjustment and do not allow the tuning of individual notes to be carried out. The coupled keys can also be too heavy for the fourth finger to operate easily.

Octave levers out of adjustment often cause playing difficulties. The opening and closing action must be certain and the holes kept clear but never enlarged. Any tendency to disturb the playing position of the instrument can adversely affect embouchure control; and if the springing of an octave lever is too tight, its use can even move the mouthpiece in the player's mouth. Excess spring tension can also strain worn keywork and cause pads to vent rather than seal the hole tightly. For lubricating saxophone keywork, medium to heavy grade oil is suitable.

The left-hand first-finger plate and the B flat *bis* key should be close together and in line when looking straight down the line of keys. The left-hand palm keys which play the high D to F notes may need adjustment to make them suitably placed for the player's hand (see *Instrument position*, Chapter 7). The left-hand fourth-finger keys which operate on to the bell of the instrument must be carefully sprung to provide quick fingering action. The springing should be set so that it is sufficient to hold the weight of the keys for low B and B flat, if the instrument is held sideways with these pad-cups uppermost. When the instrument is returned to its playing position the keys will be found to have a good action.

Saxophones can be slightly tuned by adjusting the cork or felt stops on the keys. In this way a pad can be brought closer to a tone-hole for flattening a note or moved further away for sharpening it, but this technique is limited by the fact that if the pads are too close to the holes, the notes they control will be fogged. However, corks wear and felt compresses after only a little use, so that it is necessary to check the tuning of instruments periodically.

3

The clarinet bore. The barrel. Ligature, tone-holes, pads: adjustments and maintenance. The embouchure: form, pressure, application.

THE CLARINET BORE

The diameter of the clarinet bore, including that of the barrel, is critical and even in wood it is estimated to be accurate to within a few thousandths of an inch. A popular bore diameter is 14.85 mm, 0.585 inch. The specification of other diameters, for example 14.75 and 15 mm, indicates the exactness of bore design. A large-bore instrument is the term used for a clarinet with a bore diameter larger than 15 mm. The bore diameter of 15.24 mm, 0.600 inch, is used with a mouthpiece to match, so it will be appreciated that this mouthpiece and the barrel are not interchangeable with those of the smaller bore diameter instruments, and are not, in fact, between any even less different bore diameter instruments.

The clarinet bore is polished throughout and re-polishing must not be undertaken. Any compound or contact which is likely to be abrasive must be avoided, as must the alternative of any lining deposit of dried oil or dust sediment.

Although the bore is parallel in principle and often in practice, some clarinets have it chambered, that is, enlarged at intermediate positions along its length, to assist the tuning and timbre of the instrument by adjusting development of the notes (see Figure 16). When chambering is made in the bore it is very slight and to fine limits of position, and when looking through the bore gives the impression to the uninitiated that the wavy contour is an error of manufacture when in fact it is a highly intricate formula introduced into the instrument—which needs no further attention than to be kept clean.

In straight bores as well as chambered ones the bore size is enlarged by a little gentle tapering at the top of the instrument, from about the speaker key position. Near the bottom it can be seen to open out again from about the lowest tone-hole to meet the flare of the instrument bell. These two end tapers are called the top and bottom cones of the bore, which are developed in different dimensions for the acoustical requirements of instruments. The flare of the clarinet bell ends at about 60 mm, 2.362 inches diameter.

THE BARREL

The barrel or socket section which carries the mouthpiece is the shortest section of the clarinet and is the scapegoat of the instrument. Placed between the mouthpiece sound generator and the multi-holed tube resonator, this short tube is literally the go-between for curing the tone and tuning discrepancies of these other parts. To fit the spigots on these parts, the barrel is recessed at both ends, and the fit should be just firm when the joints are greased but dry, in other words before the instrument is played. The ends of the barrel recesses and the ends of the spigots must fit without any gap between them, and the central bore through the barrel should match exactly in line at each end, to the mouthpiece and the tube bores. If the top cone of the bore is continued through the barrel for tuning purposes (in exceptional circumstances), only the difference of a few thousandths of an inch between the enlarged barrel and the mouthpiece bores is permissible. The proximity of the reed to the bore of the barrel emphasises the effect of this or other internal variations, and as fine measuring tools and gauges are necessary to probe the internal contours of the barrel, judgement must be left to the clarinet designer and tuner, because the musical product of any maladjustment is very evident to a critical ear.

Once it is established that both ends of the barrel fit and the internal bore size matches the rest of the instrument, the overall length of the clarinet barrel may be the player's concern. Generalising on the full-sized barrel of 67 mm length (for both the A and the B flat clarinets), this is seldom exceeded by more than one millimetre, and the present tendency is to supply instruments with a barrel of about 65 mm in length. This makes provision for the prevailing fashion of mouthpiece lays and/or gives the barrel shortness in length for an amenable tuning adjustment when the instrument is 'cold'—a term indicating the first period of playing, before the instrument is warmed internally by the player's breath. When it is warmed internally after a few minutes' playing, notes in the throat register will become slightly sharper and this shorter length of barrel *may* therefore need 'easing off' (also called pulling out or pulling off) one of the spigots on to which it fits, by a millimetre or only a little more, to increase the overall length and thus correct the tuning of the instrument.

If persistent low pitching continues it is unwise to fit a shorter than standard length barrel or to shorten one, without first trying alternative mouthpieces and checking small tone-holes for possible obstruction. A shorter than normal barrel (or one of inaccurate bore) will affect the tone and tuning of the notes produced at the upper end of the instrument and notes in the throat register may warm up too sharp, so that, particularly when playing across the break into the upper register, a chewing action of the embouchure develops to meet the intermittent need for tuning correction. This in turn will result in a slow playing technique and a chance for the unwary to produce a squeak. Pulling the barrel out a little as mentioned above will help towards curing such trouble, but the gap in the bore at the pulled-out joint will disrupt tuning calculations if it exceeds more than about 2 mm.

To provide a greater adjustment of tuning for special mouthpieces or for climatic conditions, an extra barrel is sometimes supplied. Suitable lengths for the two barrels in a cool/temperate climate might be a normal one of $64\frac{1}{2}/65$ mm and a shorter extra one of $62/62\frac{1}{2}$ mm. If climatic conditions exceed 27°C (75°F), the extra barrel could be a longer one of 66 mm or more.

The shorter of the two barrels can be used for the first five or ten minutes of playing time until the clarinet has warmed up, after which it is well worth while, through long playing sessions, to change to the long one and avoid a large gap in the instrument bore. In cold climatic conditions the shorter barrel may need to be used more regularly in order to play up to pitch and may, even in warmer conditions, counter the effect of a mouthpiece with a long bore, an unusual lay, a soft reed or a slack embouchure. It should always be regarded as the exceptional one of the two barrels and its use a subject of doubt if this can be associated with any playing difficulty.

To check that the length of a clarinet barrel is correct for the tuning of the instrument and mouthpiece, a testing note should be provided by an organ, tuning fork or tuning pipe. The mouthpiece must be the one for regular use on the instrument and the lay should have previously been tested. The reed should not be old or very soft.

For a testing note of A 440 or 442, whichever pitch applies, the note B in the clarion register on a B flat clarinet has the equivalent sound, so this note must be in tune with the testing note after the instrument is warmed up by playing it in a temperature of 20°C (68°F). When these two notes are played satisfactorily in tune together, the same pitched note should then be played on the instrument using the alternative fingerings of the throat register, that is, by using the fingering for note B flat plus the third side key, and again by the fingering for the note A plus the fourth (top) side key. If the barrel is correct for the clarinet all these notes will sound the same—reed, mouthpiece, embouchure and clean tone-holes permitting.

On the A clarinet the same sounding note as the test note is C, which should first be checked in the clarion register, and then played again in the throat register by using the fingering for B flat plus the fourth (top) side key, or the two top side keys if the note does not sound clear. These tests have then checked a note using the full length of the instrument (clarion register) against the same note produced using the shortest length of the instrument (throat register). The barrel affects the notes played on the short length of the instrument, as already stated, so if the throat notes are flat, the barrel is too large in length and/or bore.

If a barrel is eased off (pulled off to adjust the tuning) more than suggested, it may be a slack fit and move whilst playing, owing to the slight taper given to the spigot on the instrument. In such cases of bad fitting there is a greater possibility of leakage at the joint than seems apparent.

LIGATURE

The ligature for holding the reed in position on the mouthpiece is often a troublesome fitting. It can create strain and disturbance detrimental to the critical reed and mouthpiece relationship. The standard type supplied with most instruments has two tightening screws which draw the ligature ends together. The ligature is normally placed so that these ends rest on the reed, but they frequently fail to accommodate the reed contour as intended and the reed is instead trapped or nipped between the ligature ends as the screws are tightened, with disastrous results to the reed's efficiency.

One way of avoiding the nip is to slide the ligature round so that the screws are on the side or the top of the mouthpiece, but the solid metal of the ligature, strapped straight across the reed, is again too unyielding to be fully efficient, also the new position taken by the ligature screws

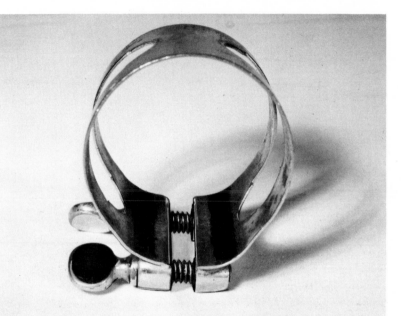

Fig. 3. **Ligature**
Along the length of the ligature, chamfer the edges (shown bright) and in the positions shown black; make the ligature fit the reed.

raises the possibility of them touching the player's face and/or being left-handed in operation. The edges of the ends of the ligature should be chamfered so that they slide over any reed (see Figure 3). This can be done by using a 'half-round' file 13–15 mm long through the ligature, along both edges and finishing the filing to a polish with number 400 emery paper.

Reeds are made of different cane thickness, and to cater for this the ligature fit on the reed needs to be variable to match the different curves on the reeds. If the ligature screw shanks or bodies are a close fit in the unthreaded lugs, reeds may be pressed out of shape or alignment because the ligature cannot adjust to the reed curve (see Figure 4). A way of providing sufficient flexibility of the ligature for the curves of reeds is to make the existing hole in each unthreaded lug into a slot, but this must retain the original *width* of the good close fit on the screw shank. A large round hole is not successful because it will allow the ligature to slip.

Thin reed position   Thick reed position

Fig. 4. **Ligature screws**
A ligature with tight-fitting screw bodies will distort when accommodating different reed thickness.

Brass screws are unsatisfactory because they may bend if the lugs are tight fitting and out of alignment, which will also result in uneven ligature tension and screw adjustment on the reed. A strong ligature is better than a thin brass one which will only put pressure on the reed at the two screw points. Strong metal carries or spreads the gripping pressure evenly along the whole length of the ligature and this gives a less harmful compression of the reed and mouthpiece. The correct fit on to the reed is that the whole length of the ligature makes firm contact as shown in Figure 3, that is, along the edges of the reed's curved surface (see Figure 3 and Plate 4).

When the ligature presses a reed too tightly on to the mouthpiece facing, the reed distorts and curls off the facing. This creates a false lay opening—the condition of an apparently longer and more open lay—which will vary with the amount of excess pressure put on the reed and the degree of hardness of the reed cane. If these circumstances still present the reed as of suitable playing strength, it might play quite well or even brilliantly for a few minutes and then become unpredictable in

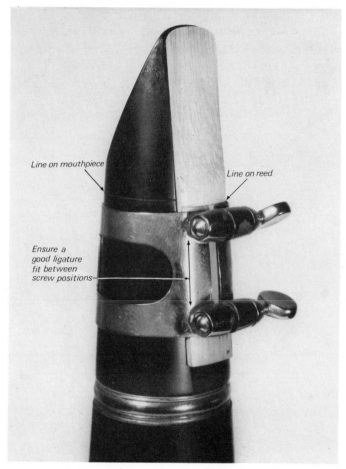

Line on mouthpiece

Line on reed

Ensure a
good ligature
fit between
screw positions

Plate 4. **Ligature fitting**

Fit the ligature to the line positions on the mouthpiece and the reed. Ensure a good ligature-to-reed fit between the screw positions.

response and unreliable in use. If uneven distortion of the reed takes place or develops, the apparent lay will be unusable and the reed may be unnecessarily condemned as unsuitable or squeaky.

Normally, the tension created by the ligature screws provides the only means of anchoring both the ligature and the reed on the polished surface of the tapered mouthpiece body. This is a bad element in design. Players are often warned against overtightening the ligature screws because this may damage the reed table, but a result of paying too much attention to this warning may easily be that the ligature is pulled right off the mouthpiece when removing the mouthpiece quickly, to change it to another instrument or to clear water from the bore on the approach of a solo during playing.

Ideally, the design of the ligature ought to be such that it is held on to the mouthpiece irrespective of screw tension and located semi-permanently in its correct position, which is shown by the rings scribe-marked on the mouthpiece. Until such luxury is provided, a lip or 'key' can be made on the edge of the ligature and a small notch cut in the top of the mouthpiece body to locate the key (see Plate 5). The notch shown is 10 mm long across the top of the mouthpiece, filed flat with a vertical edge nearest the scribe-mark to take the thrust of the key. The lip can be made by cutting two tiny slots in the top edge of the ligature 5 mm apart, and turning down the metal between them 2 mm deep. This mutilates the ligature even when sharp corners are removed, so an added key of stout copper or brass wire, hard soldered to the ligature, is preferable. When the ligature is slack, it only needs turning on the mouthpiece to disengage the key and to be removed in the usual way.

Another type of ligature has a large single screw which clamps a curved plate on to the reed. The chief failing of this model is that the plate is narrow and the reed is not securely fixed even when the screw is tight. Also, the curve of the plate does not fit all shapes of reeds, so that reeds may be cut or distorted. Moreover, if this ligature is fitted tightly on a mouthpiece without a reed in position, the mouthpiece facing can be cut and ruined. The knurled head of the screw requires a strong grip to fix or remove a reed.

TONE-HOLES

A tone-hole which is too large lets in too much air from the atmosphere to the instrument bore and this sharpens the note by terminating the sound vibrations inside the instrument bore too abruptly; while if the hole size is either too small or the lifting of its pad is insufficient to allow the correct passage of air or 'venting', the hole will give a note which is either too flat, or at least slow speaking. Consequently, when tone-hole adjustment is not possible, as when other notes would be adversely affected by it, or, as for saxophones, where the tone-holes are large and permanent in structure, any tone-hole adjustment which might be desired for correcting the musical pitch of a note frequently results in a venting compromise between easy speaking and correct tuning. In the case of different ways of producing the same note through alternative designs and/or layouts of clarinet tone-holes and the use of alternative fingerings, regard must be given to the fact that a smaller hole will allow a stronger harmonic content to develop in a note than when using a large hole. The efficiency of tone-holes is slightly altered by changes of reed, of mouthpiece, and in the volume of the notes played.

After a few months' playing, dust looking like layers of tissue will be found around the sides of tone-holes. This deposit reduces their size and so affects the tone and intonation of the notes which the holes control. Tone generally deteriorates first before tuning alteration is noticeable. Dust and loose fibres from cleaning mops and cloth pullthroughs are responsible for a lot of the deposit and much of this lodges at the inner end of the tone-holes, nearest to the instrument bore. It can generally be removed by wiping around the hole with a cloth, a screw of paper or a smoker's pipe cleaner of cotton-covered wire. A stubborn deposit may need the direct use of a reed splinter or a matchstick to remove it. A rotary motion around the inner end of the hole should be used and care taken that the bore of the hole is not bruised, particularly avoiding the top edge of the hole where the pad seats, because it is very easy to cause splintering if this is rubbed. The speaker hole especially, but also other small tone-holes in the upper half of the clarinet, may require such attention every few months of playing time to keep them quite clean. No metal tool or scraper must ever be used on a tone-hole.

If fine tuning adjustments are made on an instrument, they must be temporary, so that the adjustment can be undone without detriment to the original setting. In other circumstances such as playing at a slight change in pitch, or using a different mouthpiece or an altered lay, even a change of reed or playing volume will sometimes show that an adjustment made for tuning must be cancelled because it is not a general advantage. A change may also show that the desired adjustment can be obtained by other means.

As a tuning measure the size of a tone-hole can be altered, but this technique must be carefully considered before any adjustment is made, because, besides their own notes, some tone-holes partly control other notes (primarily formed further up the instrument) and these may be adversely affected.

To reduce the size, a hole may be lined all the way around inside the top with a ring of gummed paper or very light card. If the pitch is thereby improved but the note fogged, it may be found better to line only one-third of the hole with a tapered, narrow crescent of thin sheet cork, positioning this on the upper side of the tone-hole. Whether this lining is placed near to the top of the tone-hole, or further into it, makes a difference in the degree of its effect. The advantage in using this method is that the full width of the tone-hole is retained. After thorough testing under many different conditions an adjustment can be made permanent by varnishing the lining in position or substituting the paper by varnish alone.

Shellac flakes softened by melting in methylated spirit, as used for fixing pads, can be used as varnish. When hard, any excess varnish or surface roughness can be removed by twirling a rolled strip of number 400 emery paper two or three times on the varnish surface but avoiding the original tone-hole surface. The emery paper must not be a tight fit in the hole even for all round use, nor must it be rolled round a foundation rod for strength. No hard tool must ever be used on a tone-hole. The edges of the wood will almost certainly be damaged if these warnings go unheeded.

The sharp, raised edges of clarinet tone-holes are designed to ensure perfect seatings for the pads, thus giving quick note response and preventing loss of tone caused by tiny leaks; so any rough grain or tiny chips found on these edges must be well filled with shellac paste and the surplus removed after it has hardened. Unfortunately, the raised edges also add extra chances of leaks owing to end-play wear in the keywork. This is because a tone-hole leaves its impression on the pad and when the keywork play exceeds about 0.2 mm (0.008 inch) the pad gets out of position or 'offset' to the tone-hole, so that the impression no longer seats exactly on the edge that produced it. Distance washers to take up the wear in the keywork must be fitted in such cases.

When a tone-hole does not produce a note up to pitch, an instrument maker may 'fraise' it, that is, enlarge it only at the inner or instrument-bore end of the tone-hole. This gives flexibility to the tuning and many clarinets are made incorporating this design of tone-hole, for many if not all the holes. With this increased diameter into the bore, the small outside hole has straight-line access to a larger volume of the bore. The air column forming the note is therefore more accessible by the length, width and outwards capacity of the enlargement, which may be made directly under the tone-hole or offset according to requirements. Excess fraising adversely affects the air column for other notes. The complexities of the adjustment require much tuning knowledge in addition to the special cutters for passing along the instrument bore.

PADS

Instruments almost never need complete repadding. The repadding of a whole instrument seldom results in a desirable degree of hermetic sealing for all the pads. The consequent settling-down period is a nuisance that any player should be pleased to avoid. Only badly fitting or damaged pads need to be replaced. Small pads wear more quickly and so need replacing more frequently than large ones.

'Venting' is a term used to indicate that a pad is leaking when it should be closed (the term is the same as that used to describe a hole or key which is fully open). The fit of a pad is best tested by closing the key on to a narrow strip of thin paper inserted between the pad and the edge of the tone-hole. This is done in four or more places around the hole (see Figure 5). With the same light finger pressure, or spring pressure in the case of closed keys, the paper should be gripped equally in all places round the pad. A poorly fitting pad, which needs the use of excessive pressure to seal the tone-hole, will restrict playing to only the comparative slow speaking of notes, so playing quick short notes (as trills and shakes) on a key will test the pad by indicating the highest speaking speed.

Instrument keys are hinged at one side and this affects the distribution of spring pressure between the hinged and the other sides of the pad (see Figure 5). The side furthest from the key hinge vents more easily than the hinge side, because the extended leverage to the far side of the pad exerts less pressure from the spring for sealing the tone-hole. The fit of the pad in that position must therefore be beyond doubt. When a finger pressure is applied on top of a pad-cup and gives a springy feel, the pad is not sufficiently well seated. Skin pads, hermetically sealed in making, sometimes have excess air inside. This must be let out by making a pinprick on the underside edge, or the pads will not seat properly. On the other hand, skin with hair follicles (holes) can allow air leakage through the pad itself.

Pads should be as firm as possible, consistent with bedding on to the tone-holes, and must present a flat surface to cover the tone-holes. Any

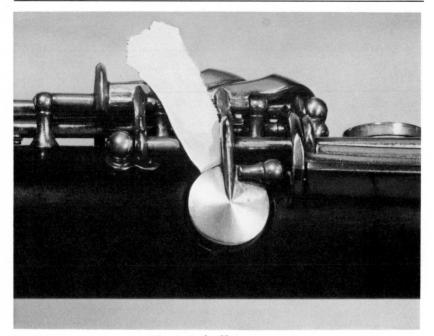

Fig. 5. **Pad efficiency test**
A pad and its tone-hole edge should grip a slip of thin paper. Test for the same tension in all positions around a pad circumference.

pad not seating all the way around, or with a cracked covering, will hinder playing technique (see Figure 6). If water leaks from under a closed pad when the springing is normally firm, this should be taken as a sign that the pad is askew or that the skin is worn or broken. A faulty pad seal becomes noticeable if extra finger pressure is necessary on the touchpiece of an open key. A lumpy surface, which develops on large pads by the felt becoming wet through a hole in the covering, is soon detected by inspection.

Clarinet pads must lift well clear of the tone-holes to ensure the true quick-speaking of notes and to avoid fogging the tone. For this reason pads must be contained within the cup diameter, which means, not to extend beyond the overall width. Pads which overlap the edges of pad-cups may, when open, still obstruct the full capacity of the tone-holes. Should fogging be suspected, play the note while closing the next tone-hole pad slightly. Fogging will then, if present, increase with the first slight movement of the key and if this occurs it is caused by this pad being set so that it does not lift far enough from the hole—obviously called 'being too close'.

When a pad has to be removed from, or fitted into, a pad-cup, a little gentle heat is needed to melt the waterproof glue which is used for fastening pads. The sticking medium is invariably based on shellac, resin or French cement (sealing wax). The key must first be removed from the instrument and should be held by a cloth or glove. A tiny flame not more than half an inch long, either from a gas cigarette lighter or similar jet, or else a small electric or other soldering iron, are suitable heat mediums. Heating the pad-cup on the outside will melt the glue in a few seconds and after removing the pad, the cup should be examined to see that the glue adheres well to the metal. If not, scratch the inside of the pad-cup to make a rough surface.

The choice of pad replacements is important if the same setting of 'sealing the hole' is to be retained. White pads covered with bladder

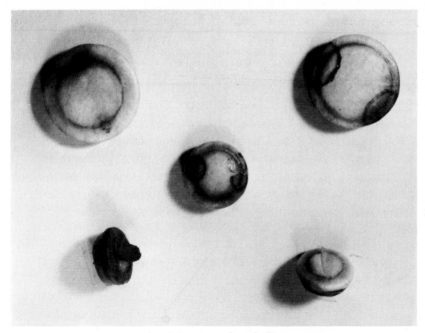

Fig. 6. **Punctured pad skins**
Sharp or rough tone-hole edges cut bladder pads, rendering them useless. A pad will be misshapen if moisture swells the felt interior. Saxophone pads are less susceptible to this deterioration.

are usually fitted on new instruments. The pad thickness varies according to style—thick, thin, double-skin covered, straight-sided, or those with a reduced size of backing card—all of which can vary the key setting when fitted in a pad-cup. It follows that if different thickness 'skin' or synthetic pads of any type are fitted, pads or keywork may need resetting to accommodate their difference. The pad backing must be full size for the pad-cup, if the pad is not to slide out of true in the crazy bell-shaped pad-cups of a clarinet. The pad backing must be kept stiff and flat, and fit into the pad-cup without distortion. A pad diameter must be larger than the hole that it has to cover, by an amount sufficient for the pad to cushion well round the outside of the hole. Besides setting the pad centrally over the hole, no fixing cement or glue should be showing round the side of the pad, as this will make the edge of the pad non-resilient at that place.

Having selected and tried the new pad for fit in the cup, put enough flakes of shellac or powdered resin in the pad-cup so that it covers the bottom when it 'boils' by applying the heat outside. Removal of the heat has to be followed *immediately* by placing the pad in the cup and holding it for a few moments by putting the pad on a flat surface and applying a little pressure on the outside of the hot cup with anything other than a bare finger. The glue sets on cooling, which can be hastened by dabbing the pad-cup with a damp cloth.

When a pad has been bedded into a pad-cup in this manner, it is advisable to reset it again after refitting the key to the instrument and checking the pad fit, even if it looks satisfactory. Reset the pad by gently warming the cup for about ten seconds and the edge of the tone-hole will bed into the pad. Care must be taken not to get heat on to the pad or the instrument, so the smallest possible flame must be used, and if this is done there should be no necessity to cover surrounding keys and cork 'stops' with a damp cloth. A very efficient way of warming the pad-cup is to hold it above eye level and apply the heat from underneath.

Pads will settle to the pad-cup rather than to the tone-hole facing and so exactness of fit between the cup and the top of the tone-hole is the answer to good and easy pad fixing—but a good fit is not always provided (see Plate 5). Unless a key has become bent and can be corrected, a pad that requires to be tipped in some direction to make it sit properly needs packing in the pad-cup. A suitable thickness of stiff card should be shaped in a thin segment to fit the pad-cup and this is glued in with the pad to lift the pad as necessary. Excessive finger pressure must not be used in bedding a pad on the instrument, as this sets the surface beyond its normal position in use and produces a faulty fit.

Dust and fine grit trapped between pads and tone-hole edges, also verdigris grown under saxophone pads, cause leaks and pad deterioration. Leather pads can be re-conditioned and cleaned with neat's-foot oil without causing them to stick. Moisture and dust will make a pad stick,

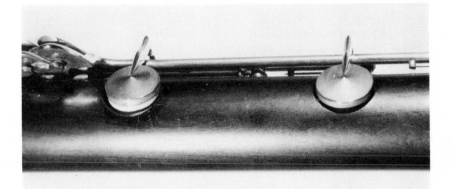

Plate 5. **Pad fixing**
Because the pad-cup does not fall central, and flat, to the tone-hole facing, the protruding pad has been positioned by inserting a packing inside the pad-cup.

but cleaning can be done by pulling a damp cloth or chamois leather pullthrough between the pad and the tone-hole. If the covering on a pad is cut through by the smooth edge on its tone-hole in only a few months, the spring is probably too strong. If the pad is heavily marked, reduce the spring tension. The roughness of wood end-grain on the opposite edges of tone-holes cuts pads in these places (see Figure 6).

After fitting a new clarinet pad or pads, the efficient seal of the tone-holes must always be tested by alternately creating wind pressure and then a vacuum in the bore of the section of the instrument in which the pad has been fitted. This is the ultimate test for tracing pad leakage and it is done on only one section of the instrument (the upper or lower 'joint') at a time.

The method is to close all the open holes and keys and to block up the bore at the lower end of the section. A cork, the thumb or the palm of the hand may be used to seal the bore, the easiest way being a well-fitting cork. At the other end of the half-instrument, wind pressure is applied to the bore by the mouth. There should be no escape of air with even a good blowing pressure. A weak spring will allow a key to blow open, in which case the movement of the key can be seen direct or through a mirror, so a little extra tension set on the spring will cure *that* leak, if the pad is sound.

In a similar fashion a vacuum is sucked in the bore. Sufficient vacuum should hold in the bore for a 'plop' to sound when the lips and the instrument are parted smartly.

Although oil applied to a clarinet bore may be prevented from touching the pads, they become affected by discoloration from the wood of the instrument. This seems to be oily and soon rots bladder (white skin) pads. Any discoloured pad should therefore be carefully examined for deterioration.

THE EMBOUCHURE

The player's embouchure is the application of the mouth and lips to the instrument mouthpiece and reed. The nature of the hold on these parts controls the speaking of the instrument in detail. The fact that this important fundamental function is not always given proper consideration, or is not sufficiently understood, can create a false impression that there must be some difficulty connected with it. Chapter 1 explains a point frequently overlooked, that every note played on a clarinet or saxophone is controlled by its particular requirement of embouchure as well as by the fingering of the instrument (see Figure 1), and this is so important to the sound, that all possible adjustments to other parts of the instrument should be directed towards simplifying the control by embouchure. It is solely the responsibility and concern of the player to satisfy the requisite standard.

The embouchure should be simply the player's own natural choice of hold by the lips for sealing the mouthpiece and reed, adding slight pressure by the jaws to bring the reed into playing position. This pressure also controls the flow of breath, to obtain its maximum use. There are two distinct methods of embouchure:

1. With the player's top teeth resting on the mouthpiece.
2. With the edge of the upper lip trapped between the teeth and the mouthpiece.

In both types of embouchure the lower lip is trapped between the teeth and the reed. The extent to which the upper lip is used over the teeth may depend on the length of the lip and the shape of the jaws or teeth, but control is better through a thin edge of lip than through the thick flesh beyond it. Wind instrumentalists' embouchures are included in dentistry study, so that a request from a player for levelling of uneven teeth or other adjustment is not considered very unusual.

The pressure by the teeth is not applied hard like a bite, but as taking hold of the reed and mouthpiece. The instrument should speak with only a low pressure of breath stream, and if high pressure from the lungs is needed to make a note speak, this must be corrected by fitting a reed with a thinner tip. The cheeks are not puffed out, but an air pocket can be formed behind one or both lips to form a cushion for the reed, and this may help in producing a soft sweet tone. The throat is kept relaxed as for singing. Taking only a short length of the mouthpiece into the mouth gives the easiest control; the amount needed to produce the lowest notes need not be exceeded. This position should play the full range of the instrument so far as the embouchure is concerned (see unbroken mouthpiece, Plate 6, and *Mouthpiece Lay*, Chapter 4).

Owing to the wedge shape of the mouthpiece, special instrument support is needed to enable the position of the embouchure on the mouthpiece to be maintained. On the clarinet this support comes from the slight upward pressure of the right thumb, under the rest on the back of the instrument, which should be covered with cork or felt for comfort. When playing notes in the throat register the player's hands have the least hold on the instrument, but the planned firmness of embouchure here for tone and intonation requirements helps to steady the instrument against disturbances of movement or twisting, which might otherwise happen owing to awkwardness of playing. Such disturbances can also occur if the spring pressure of the side keys presents undue resistance. If this happens and the pads show signs of heavy pressure, reduce the tension of the springs concerned. It is particularly important that the embouchure position and tension remain constant when testing notes for tuning or tone.

The embouchure should hold the reed close up to the mouthpiece if the player wishes to create the clarinet's particular tone of many harmonics. The lips have to be positioned on the mouthpiece in the right place to bring the reed to its working positions on the lay. In these positions a pre-determined relationship must exist between the mouthpiece lay and the strength of the reed, for the embouchure to play the instrument satisfactorily in tune. In applying the embouchure to the instrument, the first light pressure on the reed and mouthpiece should correct any slightly uneven contact between them; this is particularly necessary in the case of a new reed. The initial pressure will then have brought the reed tip to the length and tension position for playing the low register. Increased pressure is used to play the higher registers, and here some notes can easily be changed by variations in lip pressure alone. The pressure changes the length of the vibrating reed tip, and makes it possible to jump or fly from one harmonic note to another one of the same fingering (see *Bugling in Alternative Fingering*, Chapter 7).

On most instruments, a very slight adjustment of embouchure pressure is required to overcome minor mistuning of a few notes and this becomes a natural reaction with use. However, if a player senses that the embouchure has to be actually moved to another position on the mouthpiece to bring a particular note to its musical standard, instrument tuning or mouthpiece adjustment is faulty. A slight sharpening of pitch and a steadying effect on the reed are obtained by bringing the instrument close into the body whilst playing. The position increases the lip contact and teeth 'backing' for the reed, and the changed oral position gives a difference in tone.

Embouchures of more or even less than a usual length and/or pressure are used in less general playing conditions. In some instances the reason for this is perhaps to correct some fault of the reed, mouthpiece or instrument tuning. As a correction for mouthpiece rails which are out of balance, for example, one side of a mouthpiece has been put farther into the mouth than the other, as shown on the broken mouthpiece in Plate 6.

Although the lip position on the mouthpiece is considered to be constant, for extremely soft passages of music the lips can be rolled off the mouthpiece a little and the notes breathed gently into the instrument. This gives a soft clear tone of 'subtone' quality (sometimes used as a special effect in the low register) without the increase in pitch which might otherwise accompany soft playing. The same adjustment may be used for a temporary flattening of pitch during playing, until a moment can be spared for adjusting the tuning of the instrument.

During playing, the lips, mouthpiece and reed provide the seal against the escape of breath or the entry of atmospheric pressure into the instrument at the mouthpiece. Particular attention is necessary along the edges of the reed between the mouthpiece and the reed on each side, where air and moisture may collect if the embouchure is too slack. This can usually be detected because the player hears a bubbling or frizzling sound, in which case the mouthpiece and reed should be removed and

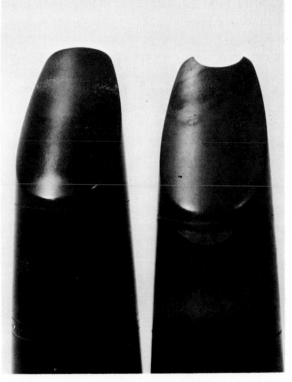

Plate 6. **Mouthpiece beaks**

wiped dry. Water alone in the reed gap is not always quite so obvious, but it holds the reed out of position on the lay and causes an immediate change for the worse in the embouchure control of notes, so should this condition develop, the same drying action should be taken (see *Condensation*, Chapter 7).

The cause of this trouble may be traced to the attempting by means of a slack embouchure, consciously or otherwise, to lower the pitch of an instrument which is sharp. Easing off the barrel, and the joint in the middle of the instrument, by from 1–2 mm each will easily cure the water nuisance, improve the pitch and tone of the notes, and allow normal embouchure pressure to be used again.

The embouchure for the saxophone closely resembles that used for playing the bass clarinet and is softer than the soprano clarinet embouchure. The saxophone type of mouthpiece lay is longer than that of the clarinet. As reeds can be expected to have an easier bending action on a long lay than a short one, this necessitates a more gentle variation of the embouchure on the saxophone. With a firm saxophone embouchure the reed usually vibrates sufficiently for the tip to touch the mouthpiece lip at each vibration. With a soft embouchure, a harder reed or less blowing pressure, however, the gap between the reed and the mouthpiece will not close so much at each impulse, and the tone is then sweeter.

When the embouchure is relaxed to give tuning adjustment, this action is called 'blowing down', which refers to the consequent lowering of the pitch. At the same time the character of the sound changes and this is noticeable in quiet music if blowing down has to be applied to any note for individual tuning. In these conditions the worst notes needing correction may not even 'speak' at all. A lowering of pitch also tends to occur with loud or heavy playing unless the player makes a correction by firming the embouchure against it. An alternative correction is to direct the strong blowing pressure on to the underside of the reed in order to hold the reed a little closer to the mouthpiece lay.

In general, embouchures vary according to the style of music, the player and playing conditions, which accounts for the variation in sound between similar instruments when played in military bands, orchestras and so on. Uncomfortable embouchure conditions, which develop from playing at poor instrument pitch or tuning, are wet on the outside of the lips, which is a result of embouchure which is too slack, and soreness inside the lips, which arises from teeth marks made by embouchure which is too tight. Exposure to hot sunshine is liable to swell the lips and temporarily affect a player's embouchure efficiency. Exposure to cold weather after playing may cause lip cracks; lip salve is a preventative.

4

Mouthpiece: materials, bore, saxophone variations. Mouthpiece parts. Lay: formation, parts, dimensions. Makers' marks. Cleaning. Graph of lays.

MOUTHPIECE

For many players the suitability of a mouthpiece depends on whether a reed will play on it or whether they are accustomed to using it. However, before giving consideration to points like embouchure satisfaction and the reed-matching form of the lay, there is another more fundamental matter which needs to be considered if the closest possible control and quality of sound are to be achieved. This is the question of whether the detailed design of the mouthpiece is the most suitable for playing with the rest of the instrument. A mouthpiece must generate specific sound vibrations and to do this it has to be made to match the instrument in several ways, so players must test this match very carefully themselves until satisfied that it provides the rest of the instrument with the best generated sound possible.

MATERIALS

Clarinet and saxophone mouthpieces have been made in wood, ivory, ebonite, slate composition, many metals, plastics, glass and so on. Facings and linings have been added in a different material from the body, to create still further variety in the hope of finding perfection for this important part of the instrument.

Wood has the reputation of giving the sweetest tone, but even the best choice of this material is liable to warp out of shape in changes of temperature and humidity and this inconsistency creates hazards that few players will tolerate these days.

Hard ebonite is the most popular material in present use. It provides good tone, the nearest to that of wood, and is unaffected by moisture. It is hygienic and comfortable to the player's lips and, if they become necessary, minor alterations to the lay contours are easily made. The sound-reflective qualities are so good that in the case of clarinets the same material is successfully used for making the main body of the instrument. Reactions to extreme temperature conditions vary with the quality of the ebonite, but although there is some general expansion with rise of temperature this avoids the warping experienced in the case of wood. In continued strong light or heat the colour of ebonite can fade and the surface become dull in appearance.

Moulded slate composition mouthpieces are a little colder to the lips than ebonite. They are consistently accurate in detail but economical to manufacture, so this may be why they are frequently found supplied on lower-priced instruments. The material has a coarser grain than ebonite, but it keeps its colour well and if proper care is taken, polishing and minor adjustment of dimensions can be carried out satisfactorily. Like ebonite, it breaks if dropped on to a hard surface (see Plate 6).

For saxophones, metal mouthpieces are in limited use where circumstances are considered to demand them, but the tone developed by metal seems to reflect the hardness of the material. When playing is started, the coldness of the metal in the mouth is distracting, but afterwards the material becomes too hot.

Plastic materials are tough and produce a tone between the ebonite and metal timbres. They are moulded, and internal shapes for producing special tonal quality are included in some saxophone designs.

Crystal glass is a substance which is unaffected by any changes in conditions and gives a good tone. These qualities have kept it popular for use in warm climates particularly. However, it has the obvious disadvantage of brittleness, and adjustments or finishing on the internal surfaces are very difficult operations.

THE BORE

Some mouthpiece bores are tapered (conical) and some are parallel (cylindrical). These two types cannot be interchanged because they belong to two different acoustical systems which in each case determine the entire design of the instrument. The conical or tapered bore produces the high notes easily in comparison with the cylindrically bored mouthpiece. The latter is used for some instruments of larger bore and in the clarion register it produces a distinctive tone, but this may be noticeably inconsistent with the sound produced in other registers. Apart from this, whichever type is used, at the point where the mouthpiece and the barrel meet, the bores of these two sections of instrument should be exactly the same.

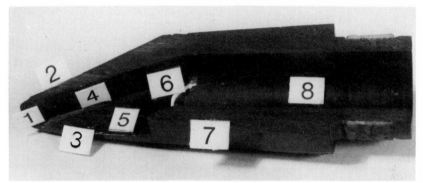

Fig. 7. **Mouthpiece parts**
1 Tip. 2 Beak. 3 Rails. 4 Pallet. 5 Slot. 6 Throat (lined white). 7 Facing. 8 Bore.

The length (depth) of the mouthpiece bore determines the upper limit of the air column in which the sounding of the notes is made. The length of the bore has therefore to be matched with regard to those of the barrel and the full instrument, so that any alteration made to a mouthpiece bore for the purpose of tuning, or for the purpose of matching the dimensions, must be regarded as an adjustment only related to the particular instrument concerned. Another instrument even of the same model will not necessarily benefit from the substitution of this adjusted mouthpiece.

Clarinet mouthpieces made to the same bore diameter do not necessarily have the same length of bore, and variations in the length will account for alterations of pitch and tone of the instrument. For purposes of comparison the lengths of clarinet mouthpiece bores can be measured by inserting a clarinet reed, thick end first, into the spigot end of the bore so that it rests across the shoulders of the slot. The length of the bore can then be marked on the reed at the point where it protrudes from the mouthpiece. Different makes or models of mouthpiece may be found to vary in bore length by 1 or 2 mm. A change of mouthpiece can therefore necessitate a change of barrel to correct the length of bore for the overall length of the instrument.

SAXOPHONE MOUTHPIECE DIFFERENCES

Older types of saxophone mouthpiece have concave-shaped sides in the slot, merging into a barrel-shaped tone chamber, and because of this shape are often referred to as barrel mouthpieces. The tone is round, clear and sweet. Instruments designed and tuned to use this type of mouthpiece require re-tuning if a different type of mouthpiece is fitted. More recent and popular mouthpieces have straight-sided slots as in clarinet mouthpieces, in order to make the tone brighter and edgy (reedy), producing a more arresting sound for little breath expenditure. Added to this, some mouthpieces also incorporate more internal resistance such as a restricted tone chamber beyond the shoulders of the slot. This chamber may be quite small and in extreme cases it is reduced to the diameter of no more than that required to accommodate the mouthpipe. But whatever the internal capacity or shaping inside a mouthpiece, it must match the tuning needs as well as the other acoustic requirements of the instrument to which it is fitted, otherwise it is unsuitable for the instrument. A close enough watch is not always kept on this aspect and as a result a desired change in tone may be accompanied by a deterioration in the pitching of high notes, or a more general low standard of tuning.

The 'reduced internal capacity' type of saxophone mouthpiece has clearly been an attempt to brighten the tone of the instrument, but the effect needs to be limited before the above deteriorated conditions occur. A moderate mouthpiece will incorporate some appreciable tone-chamber capacity beyond straight sides to the slot and this should allow a medium volume of round tone to be tunefully played (the amount may vary with the reed strength) before extra volume introduces the shriller sound. This arrangement gives provision for a fuller tonal range, after the style of clarinet subtone and full tone.

THE REED TABLE

The flat portion of the mouthpiece on to which the reed is actually clamped by the ligature is known as the reed table, to which the reed must make full contact over the whole surface, without being strained or tensioned. This fixing position of the reed is far from the sound-producing parts of the reed and the lay, so tiny faults of fit at the ligature end may be magnified several times towards the other end of the lay and cause the reed to be seriously out of position. Such faults can commonly arise from lack of proper contact with the reed table owing to

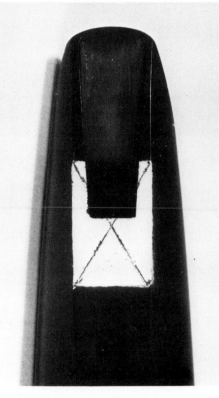

Fig. 8. **Reed table shape**

The back lay is a refinement in the form of a dished depression in the area shown white. The clarinet size of this extends from about 5 mm beyond the limit of the lay, to 43 mm from the mouthpiece tip. Crossed lines mark the centre and the position of maximum depth, which should not exceed 0.05 mm (0.002 inch).

roughness of the undersurface of a reed, or to excessive or wrongly applied pressure by the ligature. Usually, however, after some use, rough surface faults may be found to be only temporary ones, as with the assistance of embouchure pressure to counteract the minor faults, a reed will bed down properly on to the reed table and rails. The reed is then free of such trouble and if it plays satisfactorily is considered to be 'blown in' or 'played in'.

With a view to eliminating these difficulties, high-grade mouthpieces are made with an almost imperceptibly sunken reed table which can be detected as a centring feel by sensitive fingers. It can also be seen by the eye if the reed table is laid on, or almost applied to, an accurately flat surface. This sunken feature reduces the playing-in period necessary for new reeds.

Fig. 9. **Mouthpiece pallets**

Upper. *The flat type produces a bright, reedy tone.*
Lower. *The curved type produces a soft, smooth tone.*

THE SLOT

Beyond the flat reed table, the flat on the mouthpiece curves towards the tip and set in this portion there is an opening over which the reed vibrates. This is called the slot, and although its surface shape is moderately consistent, the internal shape varies a good deal in different mouthpiece designs and some of the surrounding surfaces have their own special names. The bottom or floor of the slot is known as the pallet or tone table.

THE PALLET

Its relative position and shape give it the function of creating the balance between the vibrations it reflects down the bore of the instrument and those that it throws back towards the reed. The pallet gets its name of tone table from the effect of its proximity to the vibrating reed, along with the position of these two parts and the instrument bore, which all play an important role in the production of the instrument's tone. This position-effect is also to some slight degree controlled by the angle made by the reed table along the line of the mouthpiece body and by the shape of the lay. The surface of the pallet can be flat, convex or concave in its length and is usually concave across its width, especially near to the mouthpiece bore. In this way it coincides with the bore shape where the two join. The top edges running along each side of the slot are called the rails or lands (see next section) and the sides or walls of the slot, between the rails and the pallet, vary in height according to the design; in some mouthpieces the pallet is more deeply inset than in others. The walls may be either vertical or sloping and their actual shape can be seen by looking through the bore. The position and degree of slope given to the sides and the shape of the pallet give the size and shape of the 'throat' position which can be seen as a four-sided opening from the slot into the bore.

THE THROAT

The variations in size and shape of the throat are crucial items in design and manufacture and the use and operation of the throat are best judged by a simple comparison with the human throat.

All the surfaces of the slot should have been finished to a mirror-polish, but may in fact need extra burnishing with jeweller's rouge, the finish being particularly critical on the pallet near to the mouthpiece tip, but on no account must polishing change the contours of the surfaces. If, through playing for long periods without cleaning, fur is allowed to collect near to the tip of the mouthpiece, this can produce a noticeable deterioration of tone and difficulty over speaking in pianissimo passages of music. All the foregoing details of the slot opening and its capacity influence the instrument's tone; the internal volume of the mouthpiece, in particular, must be suited to the whole design of the instrument and there is nothing to be gained by any haphazard variation of these factors.

THE RAILS

The rails of a mouthpiece are sometimes made thin in order to present less wetted surface to the reed where they are in contact during playing. This also allows the maximum possible width of reed to vibrate over the slot. There may, however, be some disadvantage, since whatever the thickness of the rails, the embouchure pressure holds the reed on to them and produces impressions or bruising along the edges of the reed. The thin rails are liable to bruise the reed more quickly and deeply so that the freshness of the reed may fade sooner than when thicker rails are provided to support it.

Another important consideration concerning the rails is that the over-all width of them should be such that their surface can be seen along the outside edges of the reed, except where the player's lips surround the mouthpiece. This useful condition is not normally provided by the makers, but the advantage of it is that the reed can be seen to be set straight and centrally positioned over the rails and this fitting has to be done frequently and with great precision. In the position where the lips are placed round the mouthpiece, the distance between the outer edges of the rails is required to be exactly the same or even fractionally less than the width of the reed, so as to enable the lips to make the fullest unhindered contact on the reed edges and in this way giving instant pressure control.

THE LAY

The curve formed by the rails or the actual shaped surface of the rails is what is meant by the general term 'the mouthpiece lay'. This curve creates the gap seen between a reed and the mouthpiece. The lay of a mouthpiece can therefore be described as the shape of the rails in the opening from the reed, or more accurately, from the plane of the lay flat described below. The flat side along a mouthpiece may appear to have a simple shaping, but this should in fact be a complex curve and, as explained in the previous paragraphs, the slot has been made through this part of the mouthpiece, which leaves only the rails to be curved in shape to form the lay.

FORMATION

During manufacture, even after the stage when the rails are formed by cutting out the slot, the lay is not shaped or 'cut' and a mouthpiece may yet be referred to as a blank, indicating that the rails are still part of the flat full-length surface, which shall be called the lay flat. From this flat blank, the end part of the rails is sloped away lengthwise towards the tip end of the mouthpiece in a very precisely shaped curve which must be formed without making any difference at all between the curve on each of the two rails.

The point where the shaping starts is called the point of lay infinity, and the rest of the flat to the furthest end of the reed table remains as the zero plane from which the lay is measurable when making or identifying its shape. However, the total length of lay gives no true indication of the length of free reed in vibration whilst playing, because the lay curve is used to change the amount of reed contact being made on the lay at any one time (see *Lay Curve* and Chapter 5 on *Reeds*).

LENGTH REQUIRED

To generate the best musical sound the lay on a mouthpiece must be long enough in practical use, which includes the influences of embouchure and blowing pressure, to give the reed freedom to vibrate at the pulsation rate to produce the lowest note on the instrument. This means that the lay must be made sufficiently long to leave a long length of reed clear of the rails, so that this can vibrate as a full-length pendulum without any other part of the lay touching the reed before it vibrates to its fullest extent. If the vibrating reed does touch the lay at some point considerably towards the tip of the mouthpiece whilst being played in the long length, the pendulum motion of the reed will be upset. The vibrations of the reed may then be halted or become impaired by, instead of free of, the mouthpiece lay. A shorter section only of the reed, if it is still free, may vibrate and produce a squeak in place of the lower note.

LENGTH CONTROL

Whatever the length of lay used to produce the lower notes of the instrument, this has to be reduced to play higher notes correctly. The lay is therefore used more or less fully length for low (fundamental) notes and shortened for the higher (harmonic) notes progressively. Theoretically, at least, the lay length is focused along the lay curve by the embouchure, to control the reed vibrating length for the note fingered on the instrument. In this way the sound generated by the mouthpiece is matched with the length of instrument tube to play that note. This mouthpiece lay control of the reed by the embouchure is a fundamental operation, higher notes being played when the free reed length becomes shortened on the lay curve to the reduced length which generates faster vibrations.

An essential characteristic of a good lay form is that it shall enable the player to exercise the necessary control of the reed by the embouchure, with the minimum of effort and the maximum of assurance and reliability. On the other hand, for all notes to be played at their best, this control can only be obtained by using a lay most equable to the instrument's requirements. Fortunately these two considerations are complementary to each other, so they do not together narrow the choice of a good lay.

Different lengths of lay and curves of course give different reed responses controlling the volume, pitch and tone of notes, so these do affect the timbre of an instrument. Correction of any of these aspects of the sound in the course of playing will be a handicap for the player.

LENGTH MEASUREMENT

To determine the point at which the curve begins, for measuring the length of a lay, a reed placed on the mouthpiece is neither rigid nor accurately flat enough to be a reliable guide. To find the start of the lay curve the reed table of the mouthpiece should be gently rubbed on a perfectly flat smooth surface. This will dull the polish on the mouthpiece flat surface but leave the lay still polished from its very beginning. The start of the lay will then be clearly seen at the place where tiny scratches on the rails mark the change from dull to polished surface.

There is variety in indicating the lay length measurement and the length from this point can be taken to any of three positions on the mouthpiece tip as shown in Figure 10. The longest distance is obviously to the very end of the tip in the centre. The second position is the point to which the centre of the reed tip extends, usually described as the inside line of the mouthpiece tip, even though on a well-used mouthpiece there is often no precise visible line just inside the tip to which the measurement can exactly be made. (This is nevertheless the best place for gauging the mouthpiece tip opening.) The third position for measuring the length is to the end of the rails, but this place again may not be very clearly defined, as the corners between the rails and the lip are generally rounded. At this position measurement can also be made of the tip opening across the width of the rails. Owing to the curve on the mouthpiece lip, this measurement will be generally 0.15–0.25 mm (0.006–0.01 inch) less than that at the centre of the tip.

For lower-voiced instruments the lay length increases according to the extra length of vibrating reed needed for the lower range. For saxophones the lay length is not quite so critical as for clarinets and an extra

Fig. 10. **Mouthpiece tip**

The length of lay measurements may be taken from the extreme tip, the inside of the tip, or the full width of the tip at the end of the rails. The extreme tip is the least reliable position for determining the amount of opening made at the mouthpiece tip.

millimetre may help in playing low notes. Although the range of the soprano saxophone is restricted in comparison with that of the clarinet, a look at the graphs on page 00 will show that the lengths of both lays are almost the same. But in order that the alto saxophone may produce the same pitch of low notes as the clarinet, its lay is cut longer. This happens on account of the difference between the respective tubular and conical styles of the instrument bores. Tenor saxophone and alto clarinet mouthpieces have similar lengths of lay, while those for baritone saxophone and bass clarinet also differ very little from each other. For each of the above ranges of instruments the increase in lay length is about 3–4 mm.

LENGTH VARIATION

If the proportion of the lay length to that of the tip opening and the position of the lay curve sections are retained, length variation of a millimetre either way (to satisfy advocates of long or short lays) should still be within the lay tolerance of an instrument, and play very successfully.

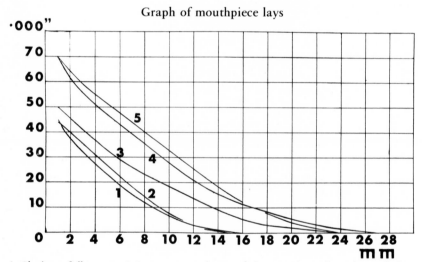

Graph of mouthpiece lays

1 Clarinet, full range. 2 Soprano saxophone. 3 Alto saxophone, barrel mouthpiece.
4 Tenor saxophone. 5 Alto saxophone, 5 star.

LONG LAYS

Long clarinet lays play expressively and powerfully. They also make for the easy tuning of notes by the embouchure and are therefore very convenient for playing smears and glissando. Maybe for these benefits some players use a long lay, called a German lay on the clarinet, which is of about the same dimensions as an alto saxophone lay. One disadvantage that may occur with such an easy variation of tuning is that the pitch of notes can easily be lost inadvertently. Another is the tendency towards intonation alteration (which it may not always be possible to correct) between loud and soft passages of music. To gain satisfactory intonation on high notes it may be found necessary to use a shorter barrel than normal, with doubtful repercussions.

Hard blowing can force the reed away from any lay surface, but on a long lay this action lengthens the actual distance more easily so that it increases the length of free reed beyond the control either of the embouchure or of the tone-holes for the notes fingered on the instrument. This may produce flattened notes or unwanted harmonic squeaks, and whether these difficulties can be avoided on a long lay will depend on the curve proportions of the lay and the accuracy of the reed scrape to match them. Long lays are best matched with long scrapes on the reed and the variations of scrape obtainable between different brands of reed can be usefully chosen in this connection.

SHORT LAYS

By comparison with a long lay, a short lay, sometimes known as an Italian lay, will give a rather higher pitch to notes, and if the shortness is carried to extremes it will be necessary, when using such a lay, to 'blow down' the pitch of some low notes if they are to be played in tune. This is an inconsistency of intonation that should be avoided. A short lay that is also 'close', which term means that it makes only a narrow gap from the reed at the tip end, will involve the player in the use of a harder reed. In some cases this may be an advantage when the reed has to be controlled for exceptionally fast tonguing, but hard reeds need more blowing pressure to make them vibrate and through long phrases of music this is much more difficult to maintain: also required is excess lip pressure for control of the reed. Constant hard blowing pressure is undesirable over a long period of time and such use of the player's lungs involves quite harsh treatment. A short lay used with a fairly soft reed is a very suitable combination for chamber music playing.

TIP OPENING

A very critical dimension of a mouthpiece lay is that of the gap between the end of the reed and the mouthpiece lip, as it is especially important that this is kept within the relation to the lay length which allows the reed to vibrate to the right intensity under all the conditions outlined in the sections on lay length and curve (next section). This dimension is known as the 'tip opening' and is measured vertically from the centre of the mouthpiece lip to the line of the lay flat. As the reed does not fit to the extreme end of the lip and this point in height is awkward to define precisely, the dimension is best taken by a feeler gauge between the inner edge of the lip at the centre, and a surface plate supporting the mouthpiece reed table. The measurement must be made in the centre because the lip is curved. Incidentally, a reed, having assumed playing shape, also curves away from the mouthpiece lip at the centre so that the aperture between these two parts is shaped similar to that at the end of an oboe reed. Such a mouthpiece lip and reed tip opening is beneficial for free blowing and easy speaking of the reed and these advantages depend as well on the polish of the pallet near the lip.

A lay with a comparatively large tip opening increases the potential volume and/or sharpens the pitch of an instrument, but for playing softly, too large an opening will result in excessive sharpness and poor tone, or even complete loss of sound. Any extreme proportion between the length of a lay and the tip opening is also liable to cause inconsistent notes in some part of the instrument's range, so extremes are to be avoided.

LAY CURVE

Even with the proportions of lay length to tip opening established, the shape of the curve of the mouthpiece rails for any one combination of these dimensions might be varied in a great many ways. In order to obtain from a mouthpiece a full and even response throughout the whole range of the instrument, it is essential that the lay curve is shaped to give, in conjunction with the reed scrape design, smooth changes in the length of the vibrating portion of the reed. In this way the reed vibrations can be easily stabilised in relation to all notes.

The curve of the rails must be accurately defined in shape and in position. Each rail must be curved to exactly the same shape as the other all the way along, otherwise the reed will not be supported equally by both rails at all stages of its progressive deflection along the lay and will give uneven response. The shaping and matching of the rails to the necessary minute degree is a skilled operation which involves the verification of the lay shape at numerous points along its length by means of an accurate surface plate and special gauges working from the lay flat level.

No reference is usually made to the actual curve detail of a lay in mouthpiece specifications. Manufacturing processes for producing very fine detail are expensive, nevertheless it is the curve which controls much of the efficiency of the lay and which requires an appropriate form of reed scrape (blade).

The curve of a lay can be examined in two halves, both of which are sections of parabolic curves with separate functions.

On the first section, nearest to the ligature position, which starts almost imperceptibly from the point of lay infinity, the curve gently increases for all of its half of the full lay. This portion is called the spring curve and it is used to slightly tension the reed to the first playing position which is used to produce the low notes. The embouchure holds the reed steady in this position on the curve, to give the correct volume, pitch and tone to the notes through the playing of which the reed is vibrating over the second half of the curve entirely without touching it.

To achieve this, the second section curve of the lay should gradually be formed as a more acute curve than the first section and it is known as the tip curve. This curve is used to support the reed when playing notes in the higher registers of the instrument in the following manner. As embouchure pressure is increased on the reed and mouthpiece, more and more of the reed length is pressed into contact with the curve, so that with each pressure increase a shorter length of reed is left free to vibrate. This action causes the pitch of sound generated to rise. When the mouthpiece lay and free reed lengths are shortened to such an extent that the reed vibrates much faster, the higher notes of the instrument's range, which would otherwise be played flat or not at all, are produced in tune because the sound vibrations generated have risen in frequency to match them.

A lay which gives a full and even response with a cane reed is made up of these parabolic segments with a flattened section between them. The graph of lays shows that for the clarinet the whole curve is more pronounced than that for the saxophone, for which the flatter portion is longer and in a different position.

DIMENSIONS

The lay dimensions and curves given in this chapter and its graphs have been chosen and proved suitable for satisfying the 'coupled reed and pipe' acoustic systems of the saxophone and clarinet instruments. Mouthpieces *precisely* made to this data will be found to play freely and correctly throughout the full musical range of the instruments. The lay lengths quoted are taken from the central point of the outer edge of the mouthpiece lip, to the point on the lay where, with the reed table flat on a surface plate, the gap between the plate and the lay surfaces is only 0.025 mm (0.001 inch). The reason for this is that a measurement taken to lay infinity is not so definite as one taken to a gauged opening. The lay infinity point would normally be about 1 or even up to 2 mm further along the lay. Tip openings are measured from the central position at the inside of the mouthpiece lip, by feeler gauges to the surface plate again in the same position, representing the line of the lay flat.

CLARINET LAY

The length of clarinet lays has varied a great deal and some are reputed to have been as short as 8 mm, others as long as 25 mm, but extremes of length such as these are not recommended for the Boehm instruments now in general use or for conventional playing requirements. About halfway between these two dimensions, however, is the length of 16.5 mm (just over $\frac{5}{8}$ inch), a most suitable length for a medium or French lay. A lay of this length will play the full range of a clarinet with the embouchure set in one position—of about the same distance ($\frac{5}{8}$ inch) measured from the lip of the mouthpiece to the furthest lip mark made by the player up the centre of the beak (slope). This mark will be a little less than halfway up the beak.

A lay length of the 16–17 mm mentioned above and a tip opening of between 1 and 1.13 mm (0.040–0.045 inch) can, with the lay curve shown in the graph, be used on both wide and narrow bore instruments. With a reed of no more than medium hardness, such a combination will ensure adequate power and complete control of playing to the finest expressions desired.

MOUTHPIECE MARKINGS

When purchasing an instrument or considering the possibility of a change of mouthpiece on an existing instrument, it is necessary to know the meaning of any markings put on the mouthpiece by the makers. In the case of a second-hand purchase it is also essential to ascertain whether or not any alteration has been carried out on the lay or any other part of the mouthpiece, in case it does not conform to the shapes and dimensions expected for its marking. There are large differences in the extent of the range of mouthpieces offered by one maker as compared with another. In one case more than a dozen different lays may be obtained for just one model of clarinet mouthpiece, while another maker will supply only a minimum range comprising close, medium and open lays.

The length of such lays would be expected to be proportionately short, medium and long. In between these extremes there are many ranges of intermediate extent. Choice is complicated by the absence of any uniform system of marking and on different makes of mouthpiece the same markings can indicate quite different lays. Marks are made up of letters, figures or combinations of both. Lays of the same dimensions might be marked C in one maker's list and S in that of another. Yet on another mouthpiece the mark C might be an initial meaning that it has a 'close' lay.

A practical point often overlooked when choosing a mouthpiece is the importance of an adequate colour contrast between the mouthpiece and the reed. The vital exact positioning of the reed is so much easier to see against a black or dark mouthpiece background than against a light one.

When playing in an ensemble, the same design of mouthpiece and lay is theoretically needed for each instrument; but for practical purposes this cannot always be applied because so many other influences are involved. Nevertheless, if intonation difficulty is encountered, it is worth trying the same mouthpiece specification for all instruments of the same bore. Even a beneficial change of mouthpiece may mislead a player on a first trial and several practice periods are required before the benefit of only a slight change in dimensions can be felt to be acceptable and firmly established.

CLEANING

Cold water with a little antiseptic added is best for cleaning ebonite mouthpieces. If a bottle brush is used for the interior, the wire end will produce scratches unless some bristles are bent up around the end and bound in that position to form a tuft. Cleaning will not wear out the lay of a hard ebonite mouthpiece unless abrasives are used. After many years of wiping with a cloth, chamois leather or other soft material, the edges of the rails can become polished or even rounded, but if carefully handled the original shape of the curve on the surface of well-matched rails will be successfully retained unimpaired.

5

Reeds: type, 'cane' Arundo donax.
Features, choice, shading. Voicing
operations and example. Strength,
playing shape and life. Squeaks.

REED TYPE

Clarinet and saxophone reeds are of the type known as beating or striking reeds which, because of their width, vibrate to beat the edges of the slot or opening over which they vibrate. On an instrument, this means that reed vibrations are limited by whatever shape has been given to the mouthpiece lay. The reedy timbre of the clarinet depends on this beating action and careful shaping of the parts concerned is necessary to produce this feature of the instrument's sound through all registers. When a beating reed does not fully vibrate, it does not make this contact with the lay and so it creates a softer, sweeter sound called subtone (see *Embouchure,* Chapter 3).

The reed works as a vibrating spring capable of being varied in length and tension and in this way the production of manœuvrable tone, easy speaking and equable pitch is made possible in all registers of the instrument. Constant deflection by embouchure pressure and variation of curvature along the mouthpiece rails (edges of the slot) demand a spring of great elasticity and resistance to fatigue.

So far these requirements appear to have been most satisfactorily fulfilled by cane, composed of hard fibres and soft organic pulp in a slightly moist state. Existing mouthpieces have therefore been developed for use with cane reeds and have not ordinarily been given a lay suitable for any different reed material. Plastic and other synthetic reeds of several kinds have been made for some instruments for many years, but have failed to find universal favour with players. Whether mouthpiece or reed development will help to improve this position is a matter for conjecture.

The other type of single reed is the free reed, which being just narrower than its slot can be vibrated right into the slot opening by strong blowing, but its tuned working length is fixed by this feature, so it is only used on multi-reed instruments.

'CANE' ARUNDO DONAX

Loose terminology abounds in the musical art and must be accepted with every possible consideration for the unusual application of words established through ages of usage. As an example, the 'cane' from which a clarinet or saxophone reed is made is really the outer layer of the large reed-grass Arundo donax. Nevertheless, instrument reeds made from this are commonly called cane reeds. There is of course a close botanical connection and the outer casing or cuticle is very hard and cane-like when it has been prepared for use on musical instruments. Again, the word reed is used for describing marsh grasses, organ pipes, the classification of several wind instruments, a vibrating tongue made from almost any substance—and so on.

The cane for making clarinet, saxophone and other instrument reeds is matured for three years in the sun to harden and ripen it, or it may be artificially dried in less time. The slowly matured cane is considered to be superior to the latter, but the quality of the cane is probably more important than the method of drying. The conditioned hardness that maturing gives to the cane should not be mistaken as being the same as that of cane which is very old or has been dried solid by over-ripening, both of which have insufficient resilience for making the best reeds. Hard cane takes the nip of a ligature without warping, but if it is too hard it does not vibrate easily enough or bed well on to a mouthpiece facing. Occasionally reeds are cut from cane which is not hardened or ripened sufficiently and these are not very satisfactory. Their useful life can, however, be improved if they are kept for some months before use.

A clarinet reed is cut from cane of 20–25 mm in diameter and the mouthpiece on to which it fits measures 25 mm in diameter somewhere just below the top end of the ligature position. Variations in the diameter size of the cane and cutting it into reeds results in different curves on the outside of the finished reeds to which the ligature has to be fitted. Every time a ligature is fitted on a reed, the efficiency of the reed depends a

Fig. 11. **End of reed, cuts**

A thin reed avoids the thick-reed tendency to be distorted by the nip of a wide ligature gap. Fit the ligature gap over the thickest place on the reed, which is often found off-centre.

good deal on the effectiveness with which the ligature adapts itself to the particular curve on the reed (see *Ligature*, Chapter 3, and Figure 11).

FEATURES

Clarinet reeds are made between 66 and 68 mm long and are $13–13\frac{1}{2}$ mm wide at the tip. Baritone saxophone reeds are almost 90 mm long and $18\frac{3}{4}$ mm at the tip, but these play just as easily and gently as smaller reeds. To form the vibrating part, about half the length of a reed is tapered, some 35 mm in the case of the clarinet reed and between 45 and 55 mm for the baritone saxophone reed. This portion of the reed is called the scrape or the blade and its exact formation to a minute detail is of extreme importance. The exact length of the scrape affects the playing qualities of a reed, for a somewhat short scrape may result in a sharper pitch being produced, or it may play only high notes 'brightly' (which means sharp and clear), but it will not be long enough to play the lowest notes of the instrument as comfortably in tune or of as good quality as a longer scrape might play them.

The line at the beginning of the scrape, which is made on some reeds by removing the outside surface of the cane in a straight line across the reed, should be used by the player as the position to which the ligature is fitted. When the reed is in position on a mouthpiece this line will approximately correspond with the position of the other ligature line to be found scribed on the mouthpiece (see Plate 4).

About halfway down the scrape, the thickness of the reed will have been reduced sufficiently for designation as the area known as the 'body', 'heart' or 'kidney' of the reed scrape, and from here to the reed end, great detail in the reed scrape concerns the instrumentalist. The reed tip is the term used for the area of the scrape extending from the extreme thin end of the reed, for slightly less than a reed's width in length. Even in this part there must always be a gradual thickening which brings the tip to merge into the thickness of the body area without any noticeable or specific demarcation line.

CHOICE OF REED

The range of notes expected from a clarinet extends from those using below 150 vibrations per second to more than twelve times that number, and every player must realise that a little effort is required to get reeds which will be capable of playing this great range of notes. Fortunately there is a good deal of opportunity for producing satisfactory reeds from many of the less suitable examples included in ready-made instrument reeds. Most makers grade their reeds by thickness, that is, according to how stiff or pliable the tip will be, but working conditions do not match those of the grading bench and reeds of any given grade do not respond consistently in playing.

Similar reed characteristics become expressed in various terms according to the different personal approaches or reactions of players. Some of the definitions used are given below with suggestions as to how these might be applied. Strong or weak (in resistance to the embouchure pressure); hard or soft (in the blowing needed to vibrate the reed); thick or thin (in comparison with a suitable tip thickness); stiff or pliable (in vibration by normal blowing); dead or lively (in speed of response).

BRAND

Variations of shape that occur between different brands of reeds include the width at the tip; the overall length of the reed—which is always adequate but may affect the appearance if compared with the previously defined length of the scrape—the length of the scrape itself and the contours of tapered and curved surface to which the scrape is cut in making. None of these factors can be neglected, as it is necessary for players to acquire the skill of recognising what combination of them will give the best individual results. As an example, although the variation in the width of reeds as mentioned above may be no more than $\frac{1}{2}$ mm, the reed must be a full-width match for the outer edge of the mouthpiece rails in the position where the lips are placed (see *Mouthpiece Rails*, Chapter 4). Besides these controlled manufacturing differences there is also the more haphazard difference of the grain in the cane. Being a natural product this does not provide consistency of material, so it varies considerably between one reed and another of the same grades or physical dimensions.

GRADE

The choice of a grade of reed will be mainly governed by the mouthpiece with which it is to be used, and the characteristics in the mouthpiece which chiefly affect the choice are the length and curve of the lay, dealt with in Chapter 4. The nature of the player's embouchure must also be taken into account: if lively passages of music are to be played freely, the embouchure must be able to control the reed without any noticeable effort on the part of the player, who must be relaxed and enjoy the easiest speaking of the reed and instrument.

Consideration for the embouchure points to a good rule of keeping reed hardness low, but it must be consistent with pitch maintenance, as it cannot be overlooked that pitch control is to some degree affected by reed strength and a reed below optimum hardness will cause playing below normal pitch. If a reed is too soft and has to be shortened by several even tiny cuts in an attempt to make it the required hardness, this will not be satisfactory because the total length and shape of the scrape will then have become too short for the reed to have a good period of playing life, or even to play well from the start. Embouchure manipulation of the reed to give pitch control is very limited in performance and is in any case a manœuvre to be avoided as much as possible. The pitch of single notes must therefore be controlled to the fullest extent by putting all other instrument adjustments in order.

To provide for these conditions and the possible variation between individual reeds it is wise to choose a grade of reed inclined to be slightly harder than may be necessary. If some scraping alteration has to be made, which is more than probable to make a reed give the best playing results, this will not then leave the reed too soft.

It is sometimes suggested that a good reed can only be chosen by playing on it, also that it should have a golden colour and a fine even grain. In fact, however, it is possible to chose a suitable reed without playing on it if the advice given here is followed. A golden colour is desirable only in so far as it may show that the cane has been nicely ripened and cured, but too much importance should not be attached to the colour of the stock or unscraped part of the reed since it is some-times stained or varnished just to give it a better appearance. The colour of the scrape is of more consequence and here any green or an overall lifeless brown colour should be avoided. The grain can be too fine or too coarse, as both qualities are required in a reed in positions and propor-tions suitable for the mouthpiece lay.

To assist initially in making a choice of reed which will need no adjust-ment or only as little as possible, a used reed which has already proved satisfactory should be referred to by the player as a pattern or guide. Present-day reeds are cut and graded with close precision, so that only slight adjustment will be needed, if the reeds chosen from the grade are those nearest to the suitable pattern.

SHADING

A reed of the correct grade does not often have its strength in the precise position best suited for vibrating on a particular mouthpiece lay, al-though after all, this is the purpose for which it is to be used. It is un-reasonable to expect every reed from a chosen grade to be ready for use in individual circumstances up to a high standard of performance. Some grain variation and thickness in the scrape where they are not wanted will be found in a great many reeds from any one grade and it is here that judgement of the reeds is wanted, to know exactly what can be easily modified.

Inspection of the grain on every reed is therefore necessary before purchase if this is possible, and buying sealed boxes of reeds is not a recommended policy. Three or four well-chosen reeds should be ample for even the busiest player because these will all have a long life. Reed 'shading' is the technique of viewing them whereby the pattern of the cane grain and the graduated thickness of the scrape are inspected by looking through the reed held against a source of strong light. Each new reed must be examined to establish whether any alterations to the scrape are necessary and possible, for giving the reed the exact amount of stiff-ness to suit the mouthpiece, together with the correct layout of grain density to give easy vibrations and embouchure control.

It must be remembered when choosing reeds in this manner that the

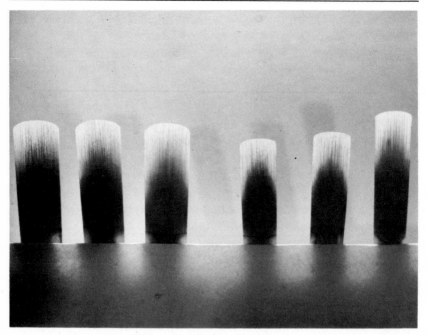

Plate 7. **Reeds (shading view)**

grain shows lighter in colour in a new reed than in a used one and the reed tip will lose most of its coarse appearance when it is dampened. The grain must run straight along the reed, with long thick fibres running down the middle to the tip end or as near as the strength of the reed allows, for the tip end of a thin reed will be thinner than only one layer of thick fibres. A few thick fibres only may be quite sufficient because these are hard and tough, but their presence and length give stability to the tip which might otherwise collapse and sound a harmonic whistle or 'tweek', at the beginning of a note, or squeak even worse if the reed is played rather dry. When played in wet conditions of embouchure or for long periods, the hardness of these fibres resists moisture saturation more than the softer elements of the cane. This saves the reed from losing springiness which would make a reed give a dull tone and be difficult to play.

The long threads of fibre also act as good carriers of vibrations from the tip, along the reed to the body section of the scrape. Their weight in the extreme tip position tends to slow vibrations there, which helps the tuneful and free playing of low notes, without the use of a longer mouthpiece lay to accommodate them, which in turn provides a simplification of reed and tone control for the embouchure. A reed to be used in a hot temperature or climate may be needed to be chosen one grade less in strength than that for use in cold conditions.

CHOICE

Remembering the suggestions already made, choose reeds with a good golden colour in the thick fibres of the scrape and notice the position of the thick fibre concentrations, which in the vibrating part are required to be mostly in the centre half of the reed's width. This may be something of an exaggerated ideal, for so long as the reed is not thicker or the grain coarser at the sides of the scrape than elsewhere across the reed, it will be a specimen of no less excellence.

This all leads to the fact that the centre of a reed must not be weaker than the sides when ready for playing and any comparatively long thick fibres towards the sides of a reed will be the ones to be first considered for being carefully scraped off or pared to tapered ends. The fibres running through the cane mostly end at various points along the reed scrape where this surface cuts through them. The long fibres left to continue to the end of the tip of the reed are thicker and more numerous in reeds of the stronger grades.

DEFECTS

There are two exceptional reed-shape defects to be considered which concern the facing or flat side of a reed. On some reeds the facing may be found to be hollow or concave across its width, either because the reeds have been cut that way or because, in drying, the soft inside of the cane has shrunk more than the external surface and formed the unwanted sunken facing (see Figure 13).

This fault is easily detected by feeling the reed between the finger and thumb. Less frequent and not so readily detected on reeds is a humped facing, that is, a slight lump of extra hard or coarse grain which has not cut level. This irregularity has more serious consequences because it does not allow the reed to fit firmly and evenly along the mouthpiece facing without causing tension in the reed. These are not insurmountable defects and action to remedy them is described later in the chapter. Occasionally the hard skin or cuticle of the cane gets included along the edges of the reed scrape. This is too stiff for use and is quite difficult to remove effectively in that position on a finished reed, so it might be considered a major fault.

VOICING OPERATIONS

Voicing a new reed includes cleaning, shading, scraping and tip-trimming operations, which may be required to achieve the individual fitting for good reed efficiency and the best quality of sound. Even though, for some players, the handling of reeds and scraper knife may be an adventurous undertaking, the importance of proper reed adjustment demands that these skills be seriously studied and mastered: the results can be highly rewarding from only a moderate technique.

The aim of the adjustments is to bring the reed scrape to an improved final thickness for the easiest possible embouchure control of its flexing action and the balanced shape of the shading which will give the very best results for the instrument. When being played, the free portion of the reed varies constantly in length and vibrations, as the scrape bends along the mouthpiece rails, through vital fractions of length towards, or away from, the mouthpiece tip end. But before the scrape of a reed is adjusted in any way at all it has to be meticulously studied in order to determine just what change, if any, is needed.

CLEANING

The reed must be well wetted and cleaned in preparation for further shading and for the following reasons. If it is clamped to a mouthpiece facing, the flat surface of a new dry reed is so comparatively hard and rough that there is no certainty whatever of it establishing the correct opening with the mouthpiece lay at the other end. All new reeds are dusty with cane dust left in the grain, which has to be removed both for playing and to enable a truer image of the grain to be seen for voicing. In addition to the rough grain mentioned above, fine cuttings of cane from manufacture occasionally adhere to the flat side of a reed and prevent the close bedding of the reed to the mouthpiece.

The wet reed is cleaned by making long light even strokes down the scrape and all the way along the full length of the reed's flat side with the knife, without cutting. This is also the way of cleaning reeds regularly during use to ensure good speaking in soft playing. After cleaning, the reed should be well wetted again to enable it to bed on to the mouthpiece reed table (see *Mouthpiece Lay*, Chapter 4).

From this time on, wetting the reed in the player's mouth is generally accepted as preferable to using clear water, which seems to saturate reeds too freely for playing condition. Any reed is moistened in the mouth for a few moments again, before and during the shading and scraping operations, to give in the first case a damp surface all over for shading consistency, and in the second case a shiny surface for seeing the exact position dulled by the knife in making a cutting or scraping stroke. The grain of a new reed, however, will take about three days to become moist and homogenised, which is its best playing condition, so it is a good idea to wet a reed once or more a day for a few days before it is wanted for voicing and use. It might also be fitted to a spare mouthpiece through this period if one is available. Damping a reed, and trying the sound from it even before voicing, helps to condition the cane and shape the reed, as well as indicating the reed's playing possibilities.

DAMPING

The flat side of a reed has more open grain than the scrape side and this may be the cause of some reed distortion until the reed has been damp long enough to acquire an even texture throughout. The time taken to develop this even texture can be very much reduced by forcing mouth saliva through the end of the reed (the heel), along the sap canals to the scrape. This is done by placing the reed end in the mouth and subjecting it to hard blowing pressure whilst keeping the end covered with saliva. The tip of a new reed usually gets wet through much quicker than the middle of the scrape and if it becomes sodden the reed should be left to dry before an attempt is made to play on it. During this wait the grain generally fills out (swells) and afterwards resists such easy saturation. Because the tip of a dry reed, new or used, takes the moisture so quickly, this early expansion of a thin tip will sometimes cause it to fold into a frill at the tip end, but this is not in itself detrimental. As the fibres and pulp in the thicker parts of the scrape get moistened through, the frilling disappears, and the time that this takes rarely delays the playing of the reed.

SHADING IN VOICING

Some new reeds absorb moisture so freely that they need rewetting after only one or two minutes' waiting time. As the shading often changes in detail during the first three or more days of moisture, voicing is best done a little each day, interspersed with playing trials, so that the reed is finally voiced after it has been dampened and played on a few times. Shading for voicing has to be done from both sides of the reed because by doing this a very slight grain variation (which can of course be on either side) can be more easily detected. Any thick patches on a reed scrape show darker in colour, which indicates strong places in the reed, so the pattern and gradation of these must be corrected and balanced to suit the mouthpiece lay.

SCRAPING

For scraping, a strong very sharp knife blade is the best instrument, because good *cutting* control is essential if the hard fibres of cane are to be satisfactorily tapered. A blunt cutting edge will need too much pressure to make it cut hard grain, which it will then chop through abruptly and create just the reed scrape condition to be avoided: a sudden end to the line of hard grain—and maybe a cut into the reed beneath it. Abrasive materials are very fast cutting but tend to cut the soft wood more deeply than the hard grain, which ruins the playing texture of the reed. However, if an unintentional knife 'nick' or similar fault has been made in scraping, 'wet-and-dry' emery paper of 400 or finer grade can well be used to grind out the error and does so almost too easily.

The scraping itself is done with small strokes made obliquely across the grain from the sides to the centre of the reed (see Figure 12). Great attention needs to be constantly paid to using only light knife pressure and to the degree of cutting, so the reed needs to be firmly held against some kind of 'anvil', for consistency. Placing the reed on a piece of glass or Perspex is sometimes recommended for this purpose, but although it is true that if a light is placed underneath, the results can be watched while the work is actually in progress, the use of such a hard support makes it easy to cut the reed too deeply. On the whole the use of the thumb and finger hold is to be preferred because the first finger under the reed provides a more sensitive anvil through which the action of the knife can be felt at each stroke. Only one small area at a time should be scraped, and a few short cutting strokes made by merely twisting the fingers or the wrist are often enough to clear a dark patch completely. The reed is then reshaded and tested on the instrument, if it looks usable.

If the reed is to match a mouthpiece with a true lay, the scrape pattern must be evenly formed on both sides of the reed's centre line, that is, the appearance of the left and right hand halves must match each other as closely as possible. Unless these are made so, the squeak-free stability of the mouthpiece and reed will be dependent on how much correction can be applied by the embouchure. Coarse or even fine grain in patches of different thickness anywhere on a reed scrape means that there will be

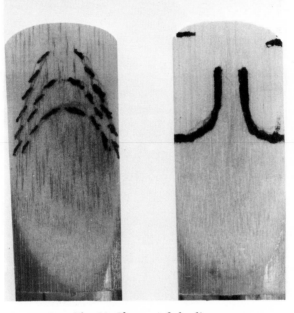

Fig. 12. Shapes of shading

Avoid hollow-shouldered shading and unequal edge-lengths. Reed-tip corners should match like a pair of bee's wings. In areas too dark in shading, make short scrapes in the direction of the dashes to produce a smooth, tapered shadow as outlined.

uneven absorption of moisture, and the consequent variation in strength and weight will upset the balance of the vibrating reed tip. An elongated pattern of shading gives easier playing of low notes than a shorter one, and a moderately thin reed gives a richer tone than a thick one.

Towards the edges of the reed scrape the shading is different from the centre, throughout the length of the scrape. The thinness at the sides of the reed tip should continue the same, or with only an almost imperceptible thickening taper along the reed scrape edges, to about the point where the open part of the mouthpiece lay begins (see Figure 14). Some alteration to a scrape to create this feature is quite common, so here is

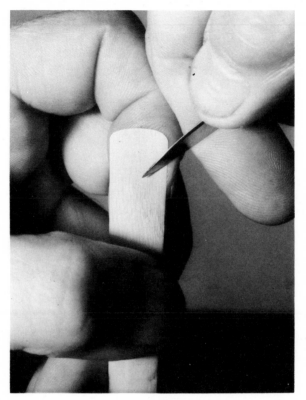

Plate 8. **Finger anvil**
The tip of the reed is always a tricky portion to scrape.

a warning not to get any element of tapering in the reverse direction, as this will spoil the reed. If this shape is not well formed over these parts and the sides of the scrape are either too thick or not properly matched one with the other, control of the reed by the embouchure will be impaired: it will not be possible for variations in lip pressure alone to make this part of the reed flex so evenly or easily along the mouthpiece rails for playing, nor to provide squeak-free stability of the reed on the mouthpiece, which often depends on how much reed correction can be applied by the embouchure (see lip marks, Plate 5). From this position (where the lay opens) along the reed, progressing to the thicker part towards the beginning of the scrape, the areas along the sides must still be evenly matched, but the tapering thickness is greatly increased.

Down the middle of the scrape, right from the beginning to the tip, the reed needs to be more evenly tapered than the side areas outlined above. Several ends of coarse grain should not be allowed to finish together in a straight line across the reed scrape; they must be reduced obliquely from each side and tapered towards the middle and tip of the reed, in the appropriate shaped pattern (see Figure 12).

REED TIP

If too much coarse grain is left near to the tip end, the reed will give a dull, wooden tone. On the other hand, if the thinning of the reed leaves the tip centre weaker than the sides, the centre will collapse under embouchure pressure and the playing shape across the tip of the reed will be lost. When the strength of a new reed is considered to be approximately correct, the centre of the tip should not be reduced by scraping, but in order to improve embouchure control, any excessive thickness or coarse grain at the sides of the tip can often be carefully tapered without necessarily making the reed too soft. The whitest, that is the thinnest, part, at the extreme tip of the reed, should be as short as the mouthpiece lay will allow. The corners of the tip need to be the thinnest part of all and to match each other like a pair of bee's wings. The centre can be kept a little stronger, where the very slightly darker shading starts to form the beginning of the longitudinal spring strength of the reed. This arrangement helps to prolong both the life of the reed and its capability to contribute to a good instrumental tone. The tip of a reed is always a tricky portion to scrape, because there is only about one layer of hard grain left and it is difficult to taper this without cutting abruptly right through the layer and into the soft grain—if there is any underneath it.

Some action to be taken in special circumstances is given below. The tip of a reed has its own particularly critical area, which is in the centre between 5 and 10 mm from the tip end, and when very high notes sound flat and are difficult to play, this part may need scraping very, very lightly to give the notes clear, free playing. The first 10 mm or so from the tip end is the vibrating portion of a clarinet reed and here every light stroke of the scraping knife needs precise control (see Plate 8). It is just beyond this position that the darkness of the shading should be allowed to increase in width more rapidly towards the sides of the reed, thus forming the body area of the scrape (see Plate 7). Another special consideration concerns this central area on a reed and the position is one which may be unexpectedly sensitive to scraping. This is about 15–20 mm ($\frac{5}{8}$–$\frac{3}{4}$ inch) from the tip end of a clarinet reed, which is just about at or beyond the position where the open part of the mouthpiece lay starts. Scraping here so quickly weakens the spring of a reed that a hard stroke or two unwarily given can make the reed unusable, but it is for the mouthpiece lay shape rather than measurements, to determine the exact pattern of reed scrape which the embouchure is best able to control.

When considering where to scrape a reed in order to give this control, it is worth while bearing in mind the relation between the mouthpiece lay length (giving the length of vibrating reed), and the dimension of the reed's width. In the case of the mouthpiece lay length of 16/17 mm suggested in the previous chapter and a reed being 13 mm wide at the tip, it is evident that when embouchure pressure is applied it will easily shorten the reed vibrating length to less than the dimension of the width. It follows from this that the reed will only require scraping within 'a reed's width' measurement from the tip end to give control on upper notes. Failure to appreciate or overlook this point may result in a loss of control for the reduction and fluctuation of the reed and lay length and this can well be a source of recurring mouthpiece squeaks.

FACING

The facing or flat side of a new reed is easiest to check when it is wet because the surface is then shiny. Some adjustment will be necessary if the reed's facing is not flat but concave across its width, or even humped in some place as noted earlier in this chapter.

A 'flat' side which is concave may still be usable on a good mouthpiece facing, if the irregularity is not excessive and the normal ligature pressure flattens the reed edges to make an efficient seal between the reed and mouthpiece facings. Alternatively, the reed can be rubbed flat on a reliable surface covered with grade 400 wet-and-dry emery paper. With a lump suspected on the flat side of a reed, the first necessity is to clean it in order that the contours of any lump can be clearly seen. This can be done by lightly scraping the flat side of the reed with a safety razor blade, which needs to be held in a clamp to make sure that it is kept flat. Any raised area on the flat side of a reed should be scraped level with the scraper knife.

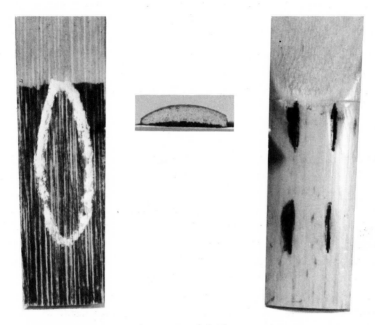

Fig. 13. **Reed facings**

Centre. *Hollow reed facings (example exaggerated) have been made for many years. They are not a reliable alternative to the mouthpiece back-lay, even if this is intended.*

Left. *Scrape flat any raised ridges or concentrations of coarse grain like that shown in the chalk ring.*

Right. *Ligature 'nips' (marked in black) often distort the reed facing.*

Many doubtful reeds can be made playable by giving them a better flat-side surface, including the area at the back of the scrape which is not immune from having long coarse-grain fibres on its surface. These will have to be reduced if they are along one side or edge only, and if along both edges, they may still need scraping instead of attempting to adjust the reed by scraping finer grain in that position on the scrape side of the reed. It is not satisfactory to reduce the scrape side of the reed when the excessive coarse grain causing the hardness is on the other, the flat side.

NOTES ON FIGURE 14

On Figure 14 an oblique line shows the positions of contact made by the reed on the mouthpiece rails when this new reed was first fitted,

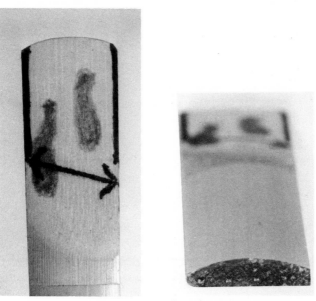

Fig. 14. **Example of reed voicing**

Reed-tip thickness 0.127 mm (0.005 inch). End cut thickness 1.27 mm (0.050 inch) on the left, 1.778 mm (0.070 inch) on the right. The scrape's uneven sides indicate the reed's thin left side. Conversely, the hard outer skin extended along this side makes the scrape too strong in this part.

indicating that one edge of the reed bedded to the facing differently from the other edge. The reed was voiced one month after purchase, when thinning the edges caused the points of contact on the mouthpiece to become nearly level at a position 17 mm from the end of the tip. The shaded patches show the areas where the too-heavy grain was also scraped off to make the shading balance on the two sides of a centre line down the reed. The tip end of the reed was 0.127 mm (0.005 inch) thick.

On this reed the sides of the stock are uneven like those of the end cut shown in Figure 13. The left-hand side measured 1.27 mm and the right-hand side 1.778 mm thick. To 'position' the reed-fitting shape of the ligature correctly on reeds like these, the ligature should be twisted round the mouthpiece a little so that the reed position on the ligature 'centres' over the thickest part of the reed. This will avoid the possible action, when the ligature screws are tightened, of pushing the reed sideways by pressing it hard along only one edge. In Plate 7 this newly voiced reed is shown on the extreme right: it is the only new reed—the others are all discarded ones which have done a few weeks of hard playing. The constant pattern of the shading on either the saxophone or the clarinet reeds, and the general similarity, should be noted.

If a reed becomes less free-playing after one or two days' use, scrutinise the scrape again for small irregularities. The correction of any tiny fault showing at this time usually re-matches the reed to the mouthpiece and embouchure. If any further adjustment is needed to aid the speaking or control of low notes, make the thinned areas along the sides of the reed scrape continue a little further towards the thick end of the scrape. For improving the freedom of high-note performance it is worth remembering the delicate reed-tip centre adjustment already explained. The golden rule is always to scrape a reed a little less than is thought necessary. Finally the reed should play effortlessly. When, after considerable use, it eventually plays a little low in pitch or feels too soft to play comfortably, the tip can be trimmed by no more than the amount of the thickness of a hair, to obtain a comfortable embouchure again in all registers. To cut 1 mm instead of one hair thickness off the tip will make the reed too hard to use.

REED STRENGTH

Reed strength is right if a natural embouchure plays a warmed-up instrument at correct pitch, but for solo playing a reed of slightly increased strength may be preferred to the one most suitable for use in small quiet combinations of instruments or for vocal accompaniments.

HARD

A reed which is much too hard can be a deterrent to playing an instrument at all, owing to the hard blowing required to make it vibrate, the poor tone it will produce particularly in the low register where the embouchure is relaxed, also the reed's slow speaking response. A reed which is just a little too hard to play freely can sometimes be adjusted to give easier blowing and normal playing, by making it lie extraordinarily close to the mouthpiece facing. The reed is given 'preformed longitudinal playing shape' in making this adjustment, which is done after well moistening the reed. The outside of the reed is placed on the hand and the upturned flat side is pressed with the thumb of the other hand, hard enough to bend the reed a little in the middle of its length. The tip of the reed must be kept clear of contact with the hand when doing this, or it will be damaged (see Plate 9). After this treatment the reed will have a 'set' and this may save scraping the reed, as it will often settle down to use without the condition of hardness returning. This adjustment is particularly effective on reeds to be fitted to mouthpieces with long lays. Hardness in a reed after a few days' use may occur owing to fur collecting on the surfaces, but this is easily removed by light scraping. High harmonic notes can be easily produced on a harder than normal reed, but such hardness is not a necessary condition: these notes can be played on a softer reed by embouchure control and with this technique the instrument's tone will be more expressive in all registers. Pitch control is indicated in the next section.

SOFT

A reed tip which is either too soft or too long reacts similarly to blowing, in that it may vibrate easily but have insufficient spring for embouchure control and this results in some notes being played only softly or flat in pitch, also the reed will not respond quickly to embouchure control. A reed must have its resistance graduated so that when it is released from a tight embouchure hold—in a shortened position on the mouthpiece lay—it will instantly spring away and the vibrating tip will lengthen. To allow this action to take place when the reed is weak, the embouchure has to be abnormally relaxed, and when the reed is blown, its vibrations overcome the light embouchure pressure and themselves lengthen the reed tip in action—which makes the notes flatter. Any reed blown so that the embouchure pressure fails to equal the vibration pressure acts similarly. The reverse action occurs with hard reeds, when an extra tight embouchure has to be used to hold the reed in its playing position and this tightness chokes the reed vibrations up towards the mouthpiece lay, where they shorten the reed vibrating tip length and create sharpness.

TRIMMING

The softness of a reed after continued use is often temporarily cured by inserting a visiting card between the reed and the mouthpiece lay, then easing the reed off the facing a little to bring the opening between the two parts back to normal, which is a correction of the excess playing

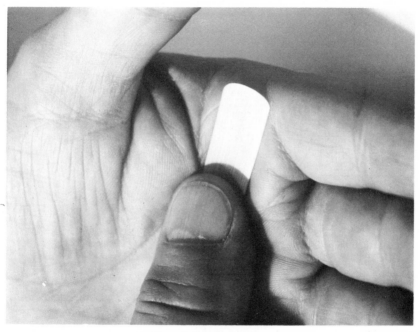

Plate 9. **Reed pressing**
The tip of the reed must be kept clear of the hand.

shape that has developed in the reed (see Figure 15). A more substantial remedy is to clip not more than the thickness of a sewing cotton thread or a piece of newspaper, off the reed-tip end.

Trimming the tip of a soft but just playable reed by the thickness of a hair alone (which is probably the thinnest cut possible) will lift the instrument's pitch and bring highest notes into playing range again if these have been lost by reed softness. Cutting the thickness of a playing card or more off such a reed tip may make the reed too hard to use comfortably. A reed trimmer called a 'cutter' is the best tool to use for judging the amount and making these fine cuts on clarinet and other small sizes of reed. An excellent reed-tip end shape can be obtained by using a reed cutter of the next size larger than the reed size to be cut. Keep the cutter clear of reed clippings because these can be only too easily mistaken for the tip of the reed when making the next cut, also their dampness causes rust on the cutting blade. Alternatively, the end of the reed may be filed back by number 400 wet-and-dry emery paper, in which

Fig. 15. **Playing shape**

The outward curvature of playing shape measured $\frac{1}{2}$ mm on a baritone saxophone reed, in each of the marked positions.

case the filing is done with strokes only from each edge across the end of the reed towards the centre.

Larger reeds, as those for baritone saxophone and bass clarinet, can be trimmed in either the same way or by a cutter, or by using a small pair of scissors and then emery paper to reshape the tip if necessary. When trimming large reeds, only very little more reduction is required than that for small reeds.

PLAYING SHAPE

New reeds need more than just a few minutes' playing to test their reliability for continuing satisfactory service. A new reed which plays comfortably, with or without voicing adjustment, is liable either to soften or to harden after being played for a short time. These variations occur because moisture affects the reed scrape as previously described, but also there is a reed-softening action of 'playing shape', taken by a reed when it is used on a mouthpiece. The playing shape taken by a baritone saxophone reed after considerable use is shown in Figure 15, and this form of shaping takes place to some extent on all reeds. Some players retard this curvature by placing reeds after use on a flat surface of glass or Perspex. On re-use the reed takes playing shape again on the mouthpiece, but only after an interim period of awkwardness in playing. As there is no knowledge of the reed's playing life being extended by this action, the straightening and re-setting procedure appears to be of little benefit.

PLAYING LIFE

Reeds last longer on a well-tuned instrument, where their springing quality is not used to excess by embouchure flexing to correct instrument tuning. Cleaning reeds as previously described prolongs their playing life, but special care must be taken in cleaning used reeds to avoid excessive cleaning along the edges of the flat side of the reed, at the places where they get heavily pressed against the mouthpiece rails. Heavy embouchure pressure or biting shortens the life of a reed, but two or three weeks of everyday use is the minimum time to expect a clarinet reed to retain its full tone and flexing capacities. Saxophone and other larger reeds are a little less critical and may generally be used for somewhat longer periods.

Either olive oil or corn oil is used as a dressing for reeds, because it fills the grain which then repels water saturation for a long period. The playing effect of oiling is similar to that of damping the reed in the mouth, the springiness is tempered, dispelling tone harshness and the tendency of the reed to squeak. An oiled reed should be used before the oil inside or outside becomes congealed.

From the first fitting of a reed until the end of its playing life, it compresses or bruises on the curve of the mouthpiece rails—a fulcrum over which it is rocked by lip pressure whilst playing. The bruising can be seen on a used clarinet reed, at the sides, centred about 10 mm from the tip end. The extent and the depth of the marks vary according to acuteness of the mouthpiece-lay curve, the hardness of the reed cane, the reed's strength at that position and the tightness of the embouchure hold.

After several days' use, a moist reed left clamped to a mouthpiece until the reed has dried may be found to be stuck to the facing. This at least indicates that the fit of the two flat surfaces is good and is not being disturbed by the ligature, although failure of the reed to stick does not prove otherwise. A wet reed will at any time *cling* to a mouthpiece facing if both of their flat surfaces are good.

The mouthpiece rails will be so far embedded into the reed after a week or so of full-time playing, that the curve on the rails will be of much less value in effectively controlling the reed's free tip length. The condition is one in which the reed is set closer to the lay of the mouth-piece, reducing the amount and shortening the length of the opening between the mouthpiece and the reed tip, which in turn reduces the reed's movement. It is unable to vibrate to the same extent as normal for loud music. The extra contact along the mouthpiece lay also reduces the reed's playing range of notes and deprives the embouchure of some reed control.

There is another springing action of the reed—beyond the embouchure position—and this is equally hampered by the bruising. In playing, the reed feels lifeless and high notes may sound flatter in pitch until the reed is trimmed and adjusted as suggested earlier. It should be noted that a well-used reed, losing its spring, may give flat notes anywhere in the instrument's range, but in doing so may indicate that some note or notes might benefit by being re-tuned. This amounts to the fact that a reed practically without spring potential is incapable of reacting to any embouchure adjustment to correct note tuning, and it must not be assumed under these conditions that note-tuning variations which arise, result from faulty tone-hole dimensions, or any fault other than the reed's poor condition.

SQUEAKS

When the tip portion of a reed is made very thin across its full width and too far along its length, the reed will 'whistle' or squeak (see *Shading* and *Soft*, this chapter). If the scrape of a reed and the mouthpiece lay do not balance in length or width and the embouchure is not able to correct the difference, there is a good chance of a squeak occurring. When the embouchure has to vary, as may happen when playing from one register into another, precise reed control can be lost and a squeak may sound. Shortening the reed by no more than the thickness of a sewing thread should improve the embouchure control and indicate whether this was the cause of the squeak. Any re-thinning necessary to the reed tip later should be done along the sides of the reed only.

A dry reed easily squeaks, so to establish the damp conditions under which a reed works inside a player's mouth, clarinet and saxophone instrument reeds are moistened and refitted to the mouthpiece facing before each playing session and then the moisture in the cane gives the reed its correct playing resilience and stability. Water between the reed and the mouthpiece lay will sometimes disturb the balance of a perfectly satisfactory reed and cause a squeak (see *Condensation*, Chapter 7). Even though a reed absorbs moisture from the player's breath, when a dry reed is used to commence playing, the absorption is so slow that, at any moment during this process, the reed is liable to prove unstable and squeak. However, in the exceptional circumstances of commencing to play on a cold instrument and urgently needing a slightly higher pitch, a reed which has not first been moistened in the mouth may overcome the difficulty. The procedure is to blow or breathe through the instrument constantly for a few minutes immediately before commencing to play (as players should always do in any case) and wet the reed well on the outside with the tongue, but great care will be required in playing the instrument during the period of instrument warming up and reed moistening by the breath.

A note flattened by the restriction of insufficient venting will sometimes change into a squeak (called 'flying') by the application of extra embouchure pressure used on the reed in an attempt to correct the tuning, but hard blowing on a loose embouchure still probably causes the greatest number of squeaks (see *Clarinet Barrel*, Chapter 3, and *Mouthpiece Lay*, Chapter 4).

6

Sound generator. Air column. Pitch.
Dynamic margin. Overtones. Registers.
Tuning. Testing. Tone.

SOUND GENERATOR

For a wind instrument to create a sound, the air inside it must be set
and maintained in vibration. This is done by blowing air into a pipe in
only very special ways, so that the blowing action generates sound-
vibrations which pass through air as sound-energy and reach much
further than anyone could directly blow through the air. Every musical
instrument must therefore have a sound generator and this takes different forms in different instruments, but in the case of clarinets and saxophones it is in the form of the mouthpiece and reed. The player blows
through the mouthpiece which includes an adjacent covering of a hole
by a thin blade (reed). The air stream of the player's breath, by passing
over the unsecured end of the blade, agitates it into vibration. This
action gives impulses of the speed of sound to the air inside the mouthpiece and to the air column inside the resonator pipe. Beyond this position, the vibrating air particles pass their energy to the air beyond the
instrument bore, as already explained in the Introduction.

The impulses of the air particles which generate within the mouthpiece are caused by each vibration of the reed completely, or for subtone
sound, almost completely, cutting off the air stream at the tip of the
mouthpiece and re-opening the aperture for it again. Pressure of the
player's lips seals the mouthpiece end of the instrument against the in-
trusion of atmospheric pressure from the outside, and also gives tension
to the reed as required for controlling it.

The formation of each of the sound generator parts, the mouthpiece
and reed, depends on the requirements of the other one, and the hold

of the embouchure around the mouthpiece must be specifically suitable for both reed and mouthpiece so that all are capable of matching the requirements of vibrations in the instrument pipe. The reed vibrates at a frequency according to the embouchure hold of the reed on to the mouthpiece lay, so the lay design must give the embouchure the scope to control the reed for any frequency of note tuned by the instrument pipe.

In contrast to the reed-instrument procedure, the flute player blows across a hole near to one end of the instrument and the blowing action causes eddies in the air stream which in turn create the impulses for sound. Another difference is that the mouth-hole of a flute remains open whilst the instrument is being played, so that the end of the instrument is not closed by the mouth as in the case of the reed instruments. This feature has a far-reaching effect, as it makes the difference known as an open pipe for the flute and a closed pipe for the clarinet. This controls quite a different combination of vibrations for the formation of the notes from these instruments, and to produce the same note an open-pipe instrument such as the flute needs twice the length of pipe to that required on a closed-pipe instrument such as the clarinet. In this respect the saxophone is again different from the clarinet, and as regards the length of pipe used for a note, it responds as the flute because of the tapered shape of its pipe bore.

AIR COLUMN

Apart from changes in the vibrations from the sound generator, the main factor controlling the fundamental pitch of the sound is the length of the instrument pipe in use. This length controls the sound even to the extent that the air enclosed by the pipe influences change in the vibrations of the sound generator. The air inside the pipe is used as a sound-resonating column and is referred to as the air column of the instrument, but it does not need to be as straight as its name implies and, if the instrument pipe is formed in bends, these do not materially affect the vibrations in the air column.

A given length of air column vibrates at a given frequency, the impulses covering this distance at the speed of sound. Shorter sections of the air column, which simultaneously vibrate in quotient steps, have proportionately higher numbers of frequencies to get the same distance in the same time, because they are taking shorter steps. If a hole is

opened somewhere along the pipe for sounding a higher note (this operation is known as 'venting'), then at this point the atmosphere intrudes
into the air column and so, for the length-producing purpose, this point
becomes in effect the end of the pipe (see Figure 16). The length of the
complete vibrating air column has thereby been reduced in length, producing a shorter air column at a higher frequency of vibrations between
the reed and this point—and this sounds a higher pitch of note.

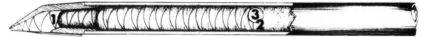

Fig. 16. **Making a note**

*Sound impulses from the reed develop along a pipe bore. The pipe length from the
throat (near the reed) to an opening, as marked from 1 to 2, is used as the distance
to create the note required from the pipe. Atmospheric pressure, at the opening
marked 3, stops further length development by the impulses.*

A whole range of notes is produced by having a number of holes or
vents which can be opened or closed to give different distances from the
mouthpiece.

This changes the effective length of the air column in the instrument
to exactly the position required for each note. Further ranges of notes can
also be produced from the quotient-controlled higher frequencies mentioned above, and when this is done these are called harmonic notes.

The principle of the length of the air column in a pipe, giving control
of the note, can be demonstrated by making the actions of fingering
notes on a pipe instrument, without blowing. If the fingers are brought
down smartly on to the finger-holes of a clarinet or the keys of a saxophone one after another, thus closing more and more of the holes from
the top end of the instrument downwards, there will be a 'plop' sound of
a different pitch for each additional hole closed. A further demonstration
is to hold down the fingers to cover all the appropriate holes for a particular note and this will give a 'plop' of the same pitch if any one or
more of the fingers is raised and re-snapped down again.

PITCH

The production of notes of accurately determined pitch and even tonal
quality is, however, rather more complicated than the simple description

just given, for two reasons. First, the pitch of a note is seldom determined solely by only the distance from the sound generator to the first opening on an instrument pipe or tube. In most cases, for practical reasons, the size of a hole cannot be made sufficiently large in relation to the bore diameter of the instrument, to determine the vibrations at that precise point along the pipe. For an opening to be efficient in producing an exact number of vibrations per second, its position and size are meticulously arranged by the instrument designer, taking into account the facts that the hole must be usable for notes in other registers, also of the proximity of the adjacent equally important tone-holes and their effect on one another. Mention is made in the overtones section of opening additional keys near the bell of the instrument—using even the C or B keys will demonstrate their effect in adjusting the tone quality on some notes formed higher up the instrument. The second reason is in the fact that all wind instruments acquire temperature and humidity from the player's breath. Since these factors are allowed for in design, an instrument does not reach playing condition until they are present. And since both of them affect pitch, the testing of pitch should be carried out well into the duration of playing periods. Provided that the temperature of the surrounding air in the room or hall—the 'ambient' temperature as it is called—is close to the standard temperature of 20°C (68°F), a clarinet will require only a few minutes' playing to warm it up and bring its playing pitch up to standard. At this temperature instruments should be at equal pitch and play together easily in ensemble, although extremes of humidity alone can upset the balance of pitch between different types of instruments.

Clarinets are less adjustable in pitch than most other instruments and their setting is satisfactory only through a very few degrees of ambient temperature. Therefore, if the above conditions do not prevail, recourse must be made to tuning adjustment, to avoid a possible deterioration in musical expression. Even so, the acceptable adjustment of a clarinet's pitch by mechanical means is limited to only one or two vibrations per second, because the adjustments cannot be made consistent on all notes. There is always evidence of a slight variation in tuning between the fundamental notes of the chalumeau register and the 'twelfth' (third harmonic) notes of the lower clarion register. This susceptibility to temperature is particularly noticeable in relation to a piano which is, in most instances, adversely sensitive. If it becomes necessary to try the pitch of a cold clarinet against that of a cold piano, it is better to test the pitch note A an octave lower on the clarinet, but owing to an anomaly of piano tuning, the lower note of A (220 Hz) on a piano is liable to sound a little sharp, so this note should not be played as a standard of pitch. The note A 440 Hz, the tuning-fork note, should be used for checking by ear other notes at intervals from it, which method can be developed to good accuracy. In cold conditions, high notes on the clarinet are more noticeably flat in pitch than the lower register notes.

By comparison, the saxophone, like all other wind instruments using the second harmonic (octave) as a sounding note, is less susceptible to temperature changes for pitch. In any case, this is more easily accommodated on this instrument by moving the mouthpiece further on or off the instrument for adjusting the length of tube for pitch adjustment. The flute has alternative adjustments, either the pipe length at the instrument joints, or the usual procedure by experienced players of twisting the instrument or only the head joint and blowing the air stream at a slightly different angle over the mouth-hole. It should be noted that a flute sounds at a rather lower pitch than normal when playing very soft passages of music and under the same conditions reed instruments tend to rise in pitch.

The clarinet is easier to flatten than to sharpen in pitch. For flattening, the joints between the various parts, mouthpiece and barrel, upper and lower finger-holed sections (themselves called 'joints'), also the bell joint, can be pulled out singly or together as necessary for the individual instrument, to give extra length to the instrument for lower-pitched notes. Half a millimetre will make an appreciable difference at a joint of the barrel. For keeping the instrument itself in tune with this extension, the 'middle' joint of the instrument may require to be pulled out more than this and the bell more again, but only if the barrel is of the correct length for the instrument, as it should be. These extensions become necessary to keep the extra length proportionate in the longer lengths of air column. When playing alongside an instrument of opposite temperature reaction, to keep all notes sounding in tune, a clarinet may require such pitch adjustments for temperature changes of only a few degrees. A clarinet should never be used when it is almost 'playing sharp', a condition liable to occur after getting too warm. This may be unnoticed until the player realises that some notes at least are being 'blown down' and the instrument has become 'woolly' or 'husky' in voice by this action; sharpness and the lack of tone are likely to become most acute in the low register.

A softer reed will also help to reduce the clarinet instrument's pitch quite considerably, because this demands less lip pressure and thus a longer length of reed will be left to vibrate. Conversely, for sharpening the pitch, a harder reed within the limits of comfortable use can be fitted. Obviously the clarinet joints cannot be shortened, so there is little more that can safely be done towards sharpening the pitch of a clarinet than to fit a suitable reed, and keep the instrument warm and the tone-holes in clean condition.

It is true that in order to sharpen clarinet pitch, a barrel of less than normal length is sometimes fitted. This is not a satisfactory adjustment, however, because although it does sharpen notes produced from the top end of the instrument, it leaves the notes from the lower end of the instrument practically unaltered. This results in embouchure instability, uneven tuning between notes, poor tone and timbre of the instrument. Attempts to correct these by the embouchure impose limitations on the player's execution. The lower half of the clarinet is also much less responsive than the upper half to the tightening or slackening of the embouchure for raising or lowering the pitch of notes and is quite ineffective in the low register. On a cold instrument, a lengthened embouchure, that is, with a little extra mouthpiece in the mouth, can sometimes be manœuvred to give a rise in pitch, but this embouchure position should not then become the normal playing position, as the lengthened position reduces the lip control of the reed. The lips should therefore be withdrawn to their correct position when the instrument becomes warmed up to its proper pitch.

It is an advantage to have a thermometer handy for temperature references when making instrument pitch or tuning adjustments.

DYNAMIC MARGIN

It is a fact that an instrument does not produce all notes at equal strength or level of sound. This is to some extent because the concentration of vibrations for a note occurs in a different position along the pipe and in relation to the open or closed holes for sounding the note. Some notes may thus be sounded slightly stronger than others, when they are referred to as privileged notes. The uneven effect of either weak or privileged notes can often be eliminated by the use of alternative fingering when it is available for these notes. This variation between an instrument's most resonant and its weakest notes is termed its dynamic margin. This factor in an instrument should be as low as possible, because the lower it is the more evenly the instrument will play, to the obvious advantage of the player.

OVERTONES

If the notes sounded by an instrument were restricted to only the fundamental notes, the range of notes from the lowest to the highest would be limited by the length of the pipe, so besides producing tonal quality, overtones in a note are made use of in other ways. Combinations of venting-holes are used specifically in order to stabilise the sound of an overtone harmonic as the sound heard from the instrument. When this is done it gives another set of notes playable on the instrument at a higher level or register, and so extending the range of the instrument.

There are various ways of inducing overtones from fundamental notes and other overtones, but on the clarinet and saxophone the 'overblowing' of the fundamental note is undertaken by the provision of an especially small hole opened by the 'speaker' key. This hole is positioned on the instrument so that opening it allows the outside air to enter and interrupt the length formation of the vibrating air column inside the instrument, which would otherwise produce the fundamental note. By this entry there is just sufficient air to form a no-pressure position in the air column of the pipe where one would not normally occur and this breaks the development of the fundamental note. The effect of the opening on the shorter, higher frequency combinations is that their numbers and shortness provide the means of avoiding the tiny inlet and the same fate as the fundamental note, so that their note is still produced and is heard instead of the lower fundamental one.

In this process there is an essential difference between the action in the conical bore of the saxophone and the cylindrical bore of the clarinet. When overblown, the clarinet sounds the note of the third harmonic, the twelfth note above the erased fundamental, while the saxophone and other reed instruments sound the note of the second harmonic, the octave note, by the same means. When using overtones in this way to produce the notes of the upper registers of the clarinet, the notes must also be specifically pitched by the embouchure of the player, as the reed vibrations or frequency (of the sound generator) assist in the exact tuning of the note. A slight tightening of the embouchure shortens the vibrating length of the reed, thus adjusting this for the higher sound and so helping to stabilise both the sounding and the pitch of the overtone.

The internal capacity of the mouthpiece tip is so small a volume in comparison with the whole amount of the instrument bore, that any lengthening effect by the change in reed length is negligible during the above condition, but the reed vibrations are greatly increased for the note frequency. In a similar manner the flat pitch of the overtone (harmonic) notes is counteracted by this slightly increased embouchure pressure. The degree of tuning obtainable depends on the player's embouchure position, the curve of the mouthpiece lay and the strength of the reed. If more sharpness is required, discrepancy in the pitch of some of these notes also needs to be corrected by opening one of the right-hand fourth-finger keys—either the E flat or the D flat one.

REGISTERS

A register denotes any voice or particular portion of the total range of an instrument, or a comparable range of different instruments, say, B flat and E flat being quoted as 'in different registers'. The term can again be applied to a tone in a multi-toned instrument, or a set of different pipes in an organ. Any of these or similar units can be called a register, but on the clarinet and saxophone the registers are small notation units of about an octave or less. The clarinet has five registers or voices, all shown in the accompanying notation diagram, with alternative names and duplicated sections.

Starting from the lowest note of the clarinet, there is the 'chalumeau' register. Its name is French, meaning 'blow-pipe', and comes from an early reed pipe called the Chalumeau, which played only fundamental notes, having finger-holes only and no speaker or other keys. As the name implies, the chalumeau register of the clarinet plays only primary or fundamental notes: its range extends from the instrument's lowest note of E or E flat up to G, the open note of the instrument. Next comes the throat or middle register, starting from this G and terminating at the C above. These notes can all be played as primary (fundamental) notes by opening successive keys until the very shortest note-forming air column of the instrument is in use. Alternatively, it is standard practice to change registers at the note B, below which the throat register might be regarded as an extension of the chalumeau register.

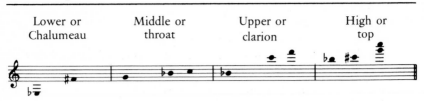

Fig. 17. **Clarinet registers and names**

From G to C in the high register is also called extreme, extended or altissimo. The closer spaced notes show the alternative fingering ranges.

There is a useful overlap about here between the throat register and the 'clarion', the next register, which is said to be the most popular voice of the instrument. This starts from the throat register on the note B or B flat and continues to C above the stave. It makes use of the third harmonic as previously described (the twelfth note above the fundamental) and is even sometimes called the register of the twelfths. The high register from C above the stave to G uses the fifth harmonic, and again some of the notes can be conveniently duplicated from the clarion register by the use of the third harmonic with the throat-register keys. Fingering in the high register needs to be carefully chosen to suit both instrument and player because of the harmonic used (see fingering charts). This need is even more acute in the extended high register covering G to highest C or beyond, which employs the seventh and ninth harmonics to sound the notes.

This extension of the register demands very reserved use because the fingering and embouchure manipulation of the harmonics are still more complex. Both the high and the extended sections are excellent for embouchure development and practice in them is a most valuable exercise. It is always necessary, however, to ensure that notes or phrases are played with sympathetically tuned fingerings, otherwise difficult or uncertain changes of embouchure may have to be made (see *Harmonics*, Introduction, and *Bugling*, Example 8).

Saxophone registers are on a much simpler scale than those of the clarinet, comprising only two in number. The first one consists of fundamental notes up to the open-instrument C sharp note, and then by pressing the speaker key for the second harmonic all notes will sound an octave higher to give a complete range of two and a half octaves for the instrument. The widening bore of the instrument and its flareless bell actually suppress the generation of higher harmonics and registers, so that the only prominent exception to the (second harmonic) rule is the high F note for which a special finger-plate is provided where the instrument bore is narrow. This and other notes using higher harmonics are thin indeed, so that although several may be played they do not constitute any register of the instrument's range. The keys played by the palm of the left hand and the side keys might be compared to the throat-register keys of the clarinet, and be considered as an extension to the register from high C sharp, with but little use for duplication of notes in the middle of the instrument's range.

TUNING

Constant listening for tuning balance between notes will show up all the tuning nuances that need correction to achieve the maximum flexibility of tuning which will accommodate a wide range of intonation conditions. An embouchure pressure variation may be necessary to regulate the different quality in octave notes, occurring as they do in totally different positions on the clarinet. The embouchure also has to adjust vagaries of tuning between the many harmonic elements contained in the instrument's notes.

If moisture is absorbed by the wood of a clarinet (ungreased end-grain at the instrument joints is particularly vulnerable), swelling of the wood into the bore can affect the tuning of notes far removed from that position. Changes in air temperature have the theoretical effect of slightly misplacing the position and size of tone-holes, and the fact must always be kept in mind that the clarinet instrument should be lengthened at the joints to accommodate the pitch of notes when the temperature is warmer than normal. The use of the E flat, D flat or other keys near to the bell for 'tempering' notes in the high register can be eliminated occasionally, but not as a rule when the playing pitch or the volume is quite high for the instrument. By these and other ways the tuning of an instrument must be adjusted a little to accommodate other instruments when playing in company or ensemble. Good intonation (the pitch of notes) is not itself a fixed pitch and will be found to wander slightly according to melodic or harmonic note classification, so that for relaxed playing, instruments must have a freedom of frequency in the expression of their notes.

TESTING

Test a clarinet by playing the twelfth intervals from the low register, keeping the slight embouchure variation for the twelfth notes consistent on each pair of notes, as between F and C and that between F sharp and C sharp, and so on. The embouchure pressure variation should feel similar for all pairs. Then test the octaves, fifths and other intervals according to ear sensitivity, finally testing steps of semitone intervals, noting for attention any which do not sound a sweet 'leading note to tonic' progression. This interval reversed may give a little different sensation of tuning or embouchure response, but there must be no 'chewing' action to correct this interval against the other. However, the leading note of any scale needs to be capable of being tempered, as expressed at the end of the previous paragraph. When testing and tuning are completed, semitone runs up or down should be smooth in tone, tune and embouchure—and then the instrument is ready for trying in ensemble-playing conditions.

TONE

Since the principal source of tone production is the sound generator, that is, the mouthpiece reed and the embouchure, every attention should be given to making these items the most suitable for the purpose, so that the rest of the instrument can make its proper contribution to a foundation that is already first class. Instrumental tone appreciation varies amongst players and periodically follows different fashions, so the question of what is right is a difficult one.

Whatever the fashionable preference, one thing is certain: an instrument must be identifiable by the same tone throughout its entire range. So a good foundation is to create an even tone, or good 'timbre' as it is called, of the whole range of the instrument. Timbre is good when every note throughout the playing range of the instrument gives the same tonal influence to the listener. Serious defects in timbre are present if some notes of a clarinet sound like a flute and others like an oboe, or some notes of a saxophone sound like a French horn and some like a motor horn.

Nevertheless, there are circumstances in which a tone varying widely from the standard timbre of the instrument is needed, and at times this is dictated by the type of music to be performed. The motor-horn reference could almost be included in the playing effects dealt with in the next chapter. They are used for orchestral effects and of course changes in the timbre of an instrument for effects are quite acceptable. The motor-horn effect is produced by using a very long embouchure to take in the use of the full length of the slot and reed. The French-horn sound is very effective and as might be expected is made by the opposite embouchure technique.

A sweet saxophone tone and a full, rich clarinet sound constitute a player's most important achievements, but any tone must be interpreted in a suitable style for the music being played, if it is to be good from the point of being in the right mood. Some of the personal inflexions used as 'mood tones' are the singing quality or style for playing ballad songs and melodies: subtone is the quality used to imply the restfulness essential for properly interpreting a lullaby. In contrast to this, very noisy music, as that written depicting battle or storm, can be played with a strident tone portraying the atmosphere of the occasion. By using these mood tones to advantage, phrases of musical notes can take on the added dimension of live expression.

The clarinet does not develop the full series of harmonics in its tone: it sounds chiefly the odd-numbered ones, 1, 3, 5, 7, etc., but these it produces in a great range, so that with a few even-numbered ones added, the harmonic 'tone' content of a clarinet note is quoted as being as high as about twenty in number. This large count provides great scope in the development of tone variation and in its use for playing harmonic registers of good quality. The accepted clarinet tone has a sound between the reedy tone of the oboe and the clear tone of the flute. Within these limits, extremes have their advocates and fashion may at times override a listener's choice. For orchestral passages a somewhat piercing tone, rich in harmonics, has the necessary carrying power: while for small ensemble and solo music a thinner, clearer tone can be used.

The brightness of tone for which the clarion register of the clarinet is well known includes strong third, ninth, eleventh and twelfth harmonics, but it is the twelfth and some other even-numbered elements which are responsible for this quality. The throat or middle register, on the other hand, is reputed to have a thin tone with little harmonic embellishment. If the notes in this register are played so that the reed-tip opening is kept to a minimum by a firm embouchure, the throat notes will be improved: but the firmness must not exceed that used for the clarion register or produce any sharp-pitched notes on a warm instrument. The use of a short barrel certainly encourages a loss of tone in the throat register, and it also encourages too much sharpness of pitch in this register, because warmth from the player's breath quickly brings this end of the instrument into warm condition without doing so further along the bore.

The flute produces a comparatively pure note containing only about four principal harmonics and this fact is the reason for the thin tonal quality of its sound. The saxophone note also includes only a few harmonics, but these are predominantly lower-sounding ones which make the tone sound rather thick and heavy by comparison with some instruments. The wide tapering bore of the instrument discourages the production of high harmonics and the fundamental note is therefore unusually prominent in the full sequence but short list of 1, 2, 3, 4, etc., harmonics. This, in fact, lists practically the whole range of prominent harmonics in the tone. For these reasons the tone lacks contrast with the human voice, which makes the instrument less suitable than most for vocal accompaniments. This instrument has suffered by being the subject of tonal experimentation and any even popular fashion in tone is not necessarily a limit to the potential use of the instrument, or the sound for which the instrument is best suited.

For some listeners, changes in the structure of notes within a scale or register give a slight variation of tone. The sound from an instrument seems to the player to be of a different quality from that heard by the listener away from the instrument. In the case of reed instruments, this is in some measure owing to the conductance of vibrations through the mouth and jaws direct to the player's hearing, which also occurs when chewing crisp food.

Tone is affected by the conditions under which an instrument is played, as, say, the pitch of the instrument in comparison with the orchestral or any slightly different pitch to which the notes must be produced. The prevailing air temperature and humidity account for pitch changes, but these will similarly affect the tone unless accommodated by re-tuning the instrument. The inside of an instrument should be kept clear of condensation as already suggested in the introduction section on sound transmission: water in a clarinet pipe reduces the fullness of tone considerably. Other sections with references to tone are those on the embouchure, reed, mouthpiece and the clarinet barrel.

Claims are occasionally made for some special reed, mouthpiece or even an instrument, that it produces a specific tone, and players may be inclined to accept that chamber, jazz, symphony, or some other kind of music, benefits from the use of such tonal specialities. Any benefits may in reality develop into a limitation for the player, by the tone being produced only in some part of the instrument or its range and possibly disturbing pitch or some other important requirement in other, or even the same, notes.

The term given to the sound heard from blowing across a flute mouthhole or an organ flue pipe is an edge tone, simply because the sound is produced by blowing air across the edge of the hole and giving the pure thin tone for which such instruments are known, but in the case of reed instruments the tone may be called edgy, meaning a reedy or rasping tone, which is of a very different character. This tone sounds more like that of the oboe instrument, with a predominance of high harmonics, and can be produced by using a tight embouchure or a soft reed on the clarinet.

A beat-tone is a phenomenon of sound developed by slightly different frequencies of sound imposed against each other. It is heard when two (or more) instruments play the same note with some mistuning, and the number of 'beats' heard per second indicates the difference between their frequencies. For example, if two closely placed instruments play together the note A 440 Hz, but one of them, out of tune, sounds at 442 Hz, the combined sound will throb or beat twice in each second. With a greater difference between two notes, the beat will increase in frequency and can resonate into a 'tone' of sound when the frequency reaches suitable proportions.

The opinion is sometimes expressed that the A clarinet has improved tonal quality over the B flat instrument, but this is not borne out by considerable long-playing sessions on both instruments. With equal use their tone tends to become similar, and it can well be that the advantageous reference to the A arises from the fact that comparison is frequently made between a dry, cool A instrument and a B flat one damp impregnated or lined with condensation, warm to a slightly too high pitch from recent use.

7
Alternative fingerings: examples, tables. Saxophone low A note. Instrument position. Transposing. Special effects. Condensation.

ALTERNATIVE FINGERINGS

The playing of passages of clarinet music, where fingering is difficult, can usually be simplified by using alternative fingerings for some of the notes. A ready choice of fingerings which can confidently be adopted is therefore an essential aspect of competent clarinet technique. The application and practice of alternative fingerings in various sequences are a most desirable part of clarinet study with a view to performance on more important occasions. Collections of music studies often include some items intended primarily for instruments other than the clarinet and these are frequently unsuitable in form and more exacting for performance on the clarinet than on other instruments, so the assistance of alternative fingerings is then welcome.

The adoption or otherwise of alternative or special fingerings is sometimes determined by personal factors such as the size of the player's hands or fingers. Such adoption, however, is not a static factor because it will change as a player's technique develops and in accordance with gradually revised considerations as to what is best for the style and tempo of the music and the precise time-value of the notes in the sequence or phrasing.

There is a large variety of other situations which may lead a player to choose a special fingering. It may, for instance, become associated with the circumstances of a particular phrase, or perhaps with the key of the music being played, thus being a reminder of the key signature because of the fingering, or vice versa.

In these last applications there will be, inevitably, a few exceptional places at which the special fingering cannot be used, but these do not usually obliterate the feeling of key sense. Using a special fingering for an accidental can remind the player that it is not part of the key signature. In arpeggios, scales or chromatic runs, different fingerings may be preferred for ascending and descending. The selection of suitable fingerings can often ease changes of register and sometimes eliminate them altogether.

Individual instruments, as well as their players, have their own particular fingering needs for overcoming inconvenient keywork movement and variations in the ease of note speaking or tuning. With a view to matching the voices of other instruments, slight differences of tone may be sounded by different fingerings for the same note. Owing to difference in the position of keywork, some fingerings on the A clarinet instrument differ from those on the B flat. The best personally suited fingering applications for all these various circumstances can be developed by inserting alternative fingerings into practice studies and testing the results.

The following series of examples will illustrate many of the points mentioned above.

For this note, use F♯ shake key: release it for D.

Example 2. Shake-key use

Side or shake keys can well be included whenever they fit conveniently into a phrase or note sequence.

Example 3. **Side-key use**

The side-key fingering for B flat (middle staff line) gives a better note on most instruments than the fingering using the speaker key, the vent of which is small and poorly placed for note production. The third side key is added to the fingering for A, to give the suggested B flat. Numbers indicate the side keys to be pressed.

this avoids thumb and finger pinch on instrument –liable to delay D.

Example 4. **Throat-register smoothness**

When the preceding and/or following notes are also in the register, B natural and C notes may be played by using side keys. Numbers indicate the side key(s) to be pressed.

open G♯,A and B keys
for high E♭.

Hold A+1

add G♯ key for D

use D + right hand fingers 2 and 3 and D♭ key for B's (×)

2
1

2
1   or 1st. finger L.H.

B♭+3

ppp

C♯ by 1st finger: thumb off hole and speaker

either C♯ or B as above (×)

slow gliss.

play this G by 'middle B' fingering:
remove fingers slowly to top

Example 5. **Keeping the same register**

Numbers indicate side keys to be pressed.

use short levers (R.H.4th finger) for quick action

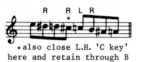

*also close L.H. 'C key'
here and retain through B

Example 6. **Left- and right-hand sequences**

Where keywork is duplicated for a note, the keys with short levers, as the right-hand little-finger keys, should be chosen for the notes requiring the quickest action. The long levers for the left hand are inclined to be cumbersome unless the springing is almost too strong for the little finger. The two fourth-finger keys for C can be used alternatively in a C to D shake although initial unevenness may occur owing to the different keywork leverages.

Fast

grip the instrument by R.H. 1st finger and thumb throughout:

in this case, the 2nd finger and thumb

close L.H. 'C key' on first note, and hold

hold L.H. 'C key' for first bar: —it may avoid 'double stops'

close L.H. 'C key' here ready for C

hold E♭ key

Fast

L.H. hold C: R.H. hold
finger holes and B

hold SK's for G♭s

Add G♯ key

hold B♭ SK: + 1st finger D

Example 7. **Fingering holding**

Whilst it is necessary to lift fingers clear of keys and tone-holes to avoid fogging the notes, there is merit in leaving fingers down or on keys which will not affect intervening notes. This extra finger contact with the instrument helps to hold it steady and reduces hand or finger movement. SK and number indicates side keys to be pressed.

keep 1st finger down through E

hold three fingers L.H.

hold B♭ SK to here. G♯ key for D

keep thumb hole closed

hold middle finger R.H.

hold SK's $\frac{2}{1}$

Example 7. **Fingering holding** (continued)

Example 8. **Bugling**

In the upper registers of the clarinet, extra lip pressure is used for changing the sounding harmonic. This can produce another note or notes on the same fingering of the instrument. A suitable term for this is bugling. Notes obtainable in this way from the fingering of B on the middle line are B, G, C sharp, E, G, A, etc. S means same fingering.

The right-hand third-finger pad can be closed to make a smooth pianissimo change of registers from C to D. If this key is closed for playing the note C, the D following in the next register speaks very freely.

Table 6. **Saxophone alternative fingerings**

Note	C♯/D Tr.	E♭	B/C Tr.	C♯	C♯	E	Top D	E	F
Palm keys								F	
							E♭	D	
					— Octave key —				
Left-hand plates	–	–	–	0	0	–	–	0	Top F plate
	–	–	0	–	0	–	0	0	–
	–	–	0	0	0	–	0	0	0
Side keys				2	2				
Right-hand plates	–	–	0	0	–	–	0	0	0
	–	0	0	0	–?	–	0	0	0
	–	–	0	0	–?	0	0	0	0
Low keys	Hold C♯ key	Move C key	When fitted			Will play 8va.			

SAXOPHONE LOW A NOTE

To play low A note on the saxophone without an extra key for sounding it, the low B flat fingering can be used when it is not required for its original purpose. The instrument can be fitted with an extension in the manner of fitting a mute to a brass instrument bell. The extension can be placed and removed, or used on a stand. For an alto saxophone the tube extension is required to be about 73×115 mm ($2\frac{7}{8} \times 4\frac{1}{2}$ inches) in diameter and length respectively. This is the size of a 16 oz baked bean or similar tin. Incidentally, the rims on such a tin are thicker, so their overall diameter is 75 mm. One end of the tube should be ringed with cork or insulating tape for fitting it into the instrument bell, which will then sound the low A note. Similarly, other saxophones can be fitted with tubes of suitable sizes, the baritone model taking a tube of approximately $4\frac{1}{2} \times 8$ inches. On the other hand, without using an extension, a low A note can be played on the alto instrument by bringing the player's left knee and the instrument bell together to use the crook or bend behind the knee as a cowl over the bell.

INSTRUMENT POSITION

To assist the continual accurate placing of fingers on and off instrument keys, the player must have steady control of the whole instrument, particularly if any important musical passage has to be performed. A firm posture curbs convulsive movement and tension which is liable to disturb critical moments of playing; it also gives confidence to the player. The position generally accepted as the most favourable is with the body upright (for breathing) and the feet placed about a foot apart, the left being further forward than the right if this is preferred (for balance). The natural head position must be established, as this will take away much tension which might otherwise be present and the arms should be held just clear of the sides of the body.

Mouthpieces should be twisted to accommodate any irregularities of the player's teeth, and the clarinet instrument can be likewise set in relation to the mouthpiece position, for the fingers to have a natural clearance of the side keys on each side of the instrument.

The clarinet should feel balanced on the right thumb, the player giving a modicum of pressure towards the mouthpiece, which enables the embouchure to hold its position on the mouthpiece beak and maintain a firm control of the balance (see *Embouchure*, Chapter 3). The alto saxophone may be held slightly to the right of the body centre line to match other instruments in a section, but a central position usually gives better control of the left-hand palm keys. Through long playing periods, baritone saxophone or bass clarinet instruments play more comfortably using a sling rather than being fixed on a stand. The slung position keeps instrument and player together with complete freedom of movement for fingering, breathing and vision.

TRANSPOSING

Some instruments are called transposing instruments and these are the ones that are made to play their natural scale at a pitch different from the piano, violin, oboe, flute, etc. This arrangement is called being at a different pitch. Pitch meaning the height or depth of the sound, it will be clear that an instrument quoted as being of B flat pitch sounds at a different height of sound from those quoted above which are in the pitch of C.

Instruments are made in all kinds of pitch, which makes them of different sizes, and to play the same sounding note as the instruments of pitch C they play notes written in a different position on the music staff lines. Transposing by the instrumentalist implies changing these positions and playing the music at a pitch different from that shown on the sheet music. This manœuvre is a makeshift procedure in ensemble playing, when one or more of the music parts is written for a differently pitched instrument from the one in hand. Transposing can be done either by using altered fingering on the instrument or by changing the music notation, with changes of key or clef as necessary. Instruments of the same pitch can of course interchange their music parts and play ensemble without transposing, but if the parts sound at altered octave levels of pitch, the originally intended effect of the music will be somewhat changed.

So a B flat clarinet plays, without transposing, music written for any B flat instrument, such as the cornet, trumpet, soprano saxophone or even the tenor saxophone. The alto saxophone, being in E flat, can use music as written for the E flat horn, the E flat clarinet or the E flat cornet, and so on.

When played on the B flat clarinet, music for the C clarinet needs to be transposed one tone higher if it is to sound at the intended pitch. The key signature will require two sharps adding or two flats deducting to complete the change (see transposition tables). The E flat saxophone requires a similar transposition for the music of horns in F. A useful way of making 'one tone' transpositions as these from printed music, is to read the upper or the lower edge of the notes instead of the note centre position. The key signature must again be altered to that of the new key note. Manuscript music is not generally exact enough for this method of reading (see Example 10).

Music for the clarinet in A, or other instrument in A, is played on the B flat instrument by flattening all notes. The original key signature is retained and each note is lowered a semitone, accidentals included. After some time this is noticed as consisting of using different fingering from normal for the written notes. The semitone lower is soon managed if it is mentally designated as the 'A' or 'flat' fingering and occasionally practised. The main hazard of this transposition arises from the fact that instruments are not so nimble in remote keys. As an example, music written in the key of G will acquire keywork complexities when transposed into the key of G flat, so that practice and care are needed to retain smoothness of execution.

change key: read note edges and play

Example 10. **Transposing one tone**

The B flat clarinet can be used to play E flat saxophone or other E flat instrument music by a transposition through the fingering of the low-register notes. This is possible because the fingering for the note G on the saxophone is of the first three finger-plates (left hand). This is also the first three finger-hole fingering on the clarinet for the note C. The difference between the notes C and G happens to be equal to the pitch difference between the two instruments, so *that* brings the sound equal for the fingering, *but* this only applies in the low register of the clarinet. The clarinet has only to be played in the low register with fingering as that for the saxophone to effect the transposition in this register. This system can also be applied to playing bass clarinet and baritone saxophone instruments (see Example 11). If the transposition goes into other registers the key signature change of one sharp or one flat must be remembered, as well as a change in the fingering, but after practice in the low register it is not difficult to follow the transposition through the middle and upper registers of the clarinet. Reversing the above method, the E flat saxophone can be used on B flat music parts, although clarinet high-register notes are not possible (see Example 12). Use of the foregoing soon leads a player to reading the transposition freely.

Alto-clef music, as for viola, is playable on the B flat clarinet by substituting bass clef and reading the notes in the same position as written, or using treble clef and reading a third higher (see Table 7 c).

D flat flute or piccolo music is playable on the B flat clarinet by changing the treble-clef sign to a bass one and adding three flats or removing three sharps from the key signature. The A clarinet is usable with music for instruments in C by making the same changes (see Example 13).

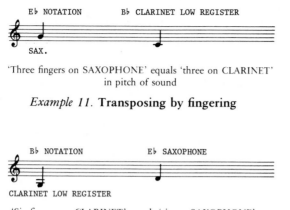

'Three fingers on SAXOPHONE' equals 'three on CLARINET'
in pitch of sound

Example 11. **Transposing by fingering**

'Six fingers on CLARINET' equals 'six on SAXOPHONE'
in pitch of sound

Example 12. **Transposing by fingering**

Example 13. **Violin music on the 'A' clarinet**

E flat instruments can be used to play bass-clef music for instruments in C, by substituting treble clef and adding three sharps to, or taking three flats from, the key signature. Accidentals must be raised or lowered as originally intended, which involves alterations to some of their characters (see Table 8 e). Alto-clef music is also playable on E flat instruments by substituting a treble-clef sign and reading one note lower than the written positions. Three sharps are added to, or three flats are removed from, the key signature (see Table 8 c).

The exceptional range of the clarinet makes it usable as an alternative for many other instruments, from the height of the piccolo down to the 'cello and bassoon. The continuous notation for stringed instruments must be phrased for breathing breaks, when played on wind instruments. When more than one instrument is involved, the omission of, or a time reduction of, a first or last phrase-note may be necessary for breathing time.

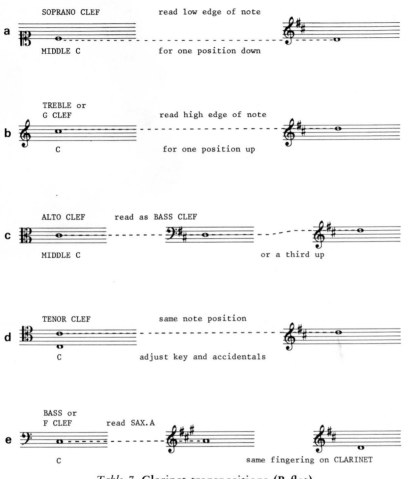

Table 7. **Clarinet transpositions (B flat)**

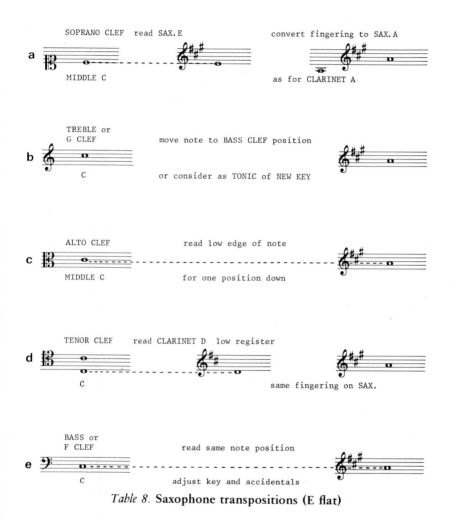

Table 8. **Saxophone transpositions (E flat)**

SPECIAL EFFECTS

At one time the saxophone was used more than the clarinet for novelty and special effects in music, but the clarinet now fully shares these features. Names and playing methods are given below and the musical signs are shown in Table 9.

(a) *Bend.* Short dips by embouchure undulations, using the articulation Ya, Ya or Yo, Yo.

(b) *Lip slur.* The lips make a smooth rise and fall of the sound. The lower note is not fingered on the instrument; the higher one is fingered and flattened by a slacker embouchure.

(c) *Gliss* (an abbreviation for glissando). This may be written in chromatic or scale notation, or with starting and finishing notes only, or with one note and the player's discretion as to length and timing. The glissando is used up or down in widely varying proportions and duration.

'*Push*'. A push gliss is strongly played, with increasing embouchure pressure on the first note forcing its pitch up towards the next note. Marked 'push'.

(d) *Fall.* A lip gliss down, without determination by another note. It should not encroach on to the following note or rest.

(e) *Lick or lift.* A short upward gliss by the lips, *from* the note after striking it.

(f) *Smear.* A chromatic notation may be given for this, or a note only. It is an embouchure-and-fingering assisted dip and return of at least a semitone. This is longer and more marked than the bend.

(g) *Lip up.* A short gliss before and *up to* a note.

(h) *Lip shake or turn.* This is often only indicated by the usual turn sign; 'lip' is not always specified. The lip movement is similar to, but faster than that for a lip slur. The rising and falling of the tongue in the oral cavity aids the turn.

(i) *Rip.* A crescendo gliss ending with a loud struck note.

(j) *Laugh.* One or more short falls from a high note, followed by others on notes descending in semitones or tones.

(k) *Vibrato.* This may be shown as a lip shake and/or written 'vib'. The end of the vibrato passage can be marked 'no vib' or 0.

(l) *Flutter tongue.* As rolling R's, the tongue flutters in the mouth.

(m) *Slap tongue.* Used on low notes to best effect, it is produced by creating a smack inside the mouth. By sucking a vacuum between the tongue and the roof of the mouth, the tongue can be made to stick to the pallet. When it is suddenly withdrawn a smack occurs and this is the principle in slap tongue. It is played by using the reed as the pallet of the mouth, starting each note by the slapping effect. The reed, slapping up to the mouthpiece from its drawn-away position, makes a loud thump when this is amplified through the instrument.

Table 9. **Special effects**

Table 9. **Special effects** (continued)

CONDENSATION

One of the results of playing reed-and-pipe instruments is that moisture collects in both the mouthpiece and the pipe, which is a hindrance to playing. Keeping these parts (of the clarinet in particular) free from water is an added duty for the player. When a player's warm breath passes into a comparatively cold mouthpiece the moisture is liable to condense into blobs and then trickles of water. This sometimes gets into the opening between the reed and the mouthpiece, when it upsets the reed vibrations, especially if the water is along one rail of the mouthpiece, as this unbalances the mouthpiece lay, to the extent of causing a squeak from the reed.

If the mouthpiece and the upper section of the clarinet bore become lined with water, which for some players is not an uncommon occurrence, there is a tendency for the instrument to play notes sharper in pitch than usual. Reducing embouchure pressure to eliminate the sharpness will allow water on the reed to enter the gap between mouthpiece and reed referred to above, with the resultant squeak or at least frying-pan noises as the water bubbles in the gap.

To wipe out the water and restore a polished condition to the mouthpiece and instrument bore, a pullthrough is a necessary accessory. This is made up of either a piece of chamois leather or absorbent cloth which is not lint-shedding in nature, attached to a weighted line or string. All of this must be small enough to pass through the instrument, but be large enough to wipe the bore clean in doing so. If the chamois leather gets stiff (hard), rinsing it in water with a few drops of glycerine added will soften it for an almost indefinite period. This saves having to use it damp, from which condition the leather soon rots. Chamois leather absorbs the water better than some fabrics may do, but light fabric in the form of a cotton or linen handkerchief is an efficient absorbent and will also polish the bore of the instrument perfectly.

Use a pullthrough from the top of a clarinet only, so that any spread of the moisture is made further down the bore to equalise the damp condition. Also, if the pullthrough jams on the speaker-hole tube that sticks out into the bore, the material can be easily removed, but if started at the bell of the instrument, a jammed pullthrough can be a difficult problem for removal, involving serious time loss and even instrument damage before it is cleared.

In addition to affecting the clarinet mouthpiece and bore, water occasionally gets carried by vibrations into tone-hole passages and these are not always easy to dry out. A tone-hole may be blocked quite completely, or water may persistently cling to the tone-hole bore and create a partial stoppage. In either case, direct hard blowing through the tone-hole several times may be needed to clear it of water, after which the instrument bore must be pulled through to clear the water from the vicinity of the hole, or it will return.

The C sharp/G sharp key almost on the underside of the clarinet is notorious for water-blobs, to use the general term, and must have ruined millions of musical passages. This trouble is overcome by the improved Boehm model of clarinet, because the G sharp tone-hole is differently placed. It is re-designed on the top or front of the instrument in a position for producing a better-sounding note and in this keywork feature alone the standard model of instrument is quite out of date (see Chapter 2). Pads can be dried by passing the pullthrough fabric over the surface, or water can be blotted up with paper, 'cigarette' paper being a favourite medium. Clarinet 'pegs' for providing stability when instruments are stood on end help to drain them of water and prevent it settling into tone-holes. Incidentally, the pegs are easiest to see if they are light in colour, which may seem to be a fine point, but it is important at times that the peg or an instrument stand should be located quickly without effort and with certainty.

The only condensation trouble beyond the mouthpiece on saxophones is the water in the 'speaker' holes and the palm-key tone-holes, with an occasional pad sticking down on a tone-hole after being damp. Even so, a stand for an instrument is a very necessary fitting. Water finding its way on to the keywork of an instrument demands immediate counteraction by the use of the oilcan against rust on rods, hinge pins and springs, and it is surprising how much the oiling benefits the keywork action.

Alto and tenor saxophone instruments as well as their mouthpieces and crooks can be pulled through by dropping the weighted line into the bottom of the bell and turning the instrument upside down. The crook, cleaned with a bottle brush, should be dried and polished to get the best playing response. To avoid condensation forming freely inside instruments, they should be brought to playing temperature if possible, without recourse to blowing through them. The swelling of clarinet instrument joints by water is prevented by greasing them with a good waterproof grease. This also helps to provide an airtight seal at the joints and preserves the cork inserts from the wear of excess friction by allowing the instrument to be assembled and dismantled easily.

A grease which keeps cork and other joints in excellent condition is made by clarifying mutton fat and adding in volume one-eighth or more of petroleum jelly. Alternatively, the purchase of a tube of lip salve, a colourless lipstick, is more convenient. This is used by wind-instrument players to prevent outdoor weather drying or hardening their lips, for which use it is also now recommended.